Grace of Giving

# Grace of Giving

*Turning the key to enter and experience fullness of life*

THE TEN COMMANDMENTS SERIES

## Marja Verschoor-Meijers

*The thief comes only in order to steal, kill, and destroy. I have come in order that you might have life – life in all its fullness.*

**John 10:10**

# Tabel of contents

# Introduction

*There is more happiness in giving than in receiving.*

**Acts 20:35**

Do not steal! Without a doubt, the shortest of the Ten Commandments and also one that does not require a degree in theology to be understood. I had, however, a practical but nonetheless burning question for the Lord when I was getting ready to work on this book: 'Is it possible to write a book about three words?'

After all, most people know stealing is unlawful; what is there to be added? I started off with a blank page, three little words in my mind: 'do not steal,' and a desperate request for fresh insights on this commandment.

As can be understood from my previous books, it is my desire to shift the focus from what we shouldn't do, to what we can do; from keeping the letter of the Law to following the guidance of the Spirit. During prayer, I was inspired by the wonderful scripture of John 10:10 and began using it as a foundation for my writing because it so unmistakably speaks of stealing and giving, negative versus positive, warning versus promise.

I have taken that scripture and split it up in three parts:

## The Warning

First of all Jesus explains what the thief is trying to do here on earth (to *steal*, kill, and destroy).

## The Grace

Second, Jesus explains what He Himself came to do here on earth (to *give* us life).

## The Promise

Third, Jesus explains what kind of life that would be for us here on earth (*life* in all its fullness).

Slowly, yet clearly, it turned out to be a book about the opposite of stealing, namely giving. It is one thing to claim we do not steal, but logical questions would be: What *do* we do? How do we go from merely obeying such a command to fulfilling it in our daily lives? How do we apply such a principle without being legalistic or too focused on wrongdoing? What action does Jesus require from us?

Giving is an attitude of love and love is the fulfillment of the Law. I hope and pray that while reading this book you will transform your thinking from the way of the thief (taking) to the way of the Master (giving). During that process, many questions will be answered, such as: Is it possible to become a giver without struggling to let go of our possessions, time, and money? Why is it we are so focused on accumulating more for ourselves? Why is it often difficult to give away freely? What can we learn from Jesus's opinion on the subject? What is the main thought behind the eighth commandment for the new covenant believer?

It will help you to pray the following words before you start reading:

*Dear Father in heaven, thank You for giving me Your Word. I want to be open-minded for what You are about to teach me. Holy Spirit, touch my heart and open my ears. In the name of Jesus, I pray this. Amen.*

*Marja Verschoor-Meijers*

# 8th Commandment

*Do not steal*

**Exodus 20:15**

# Part I

# The Warning

*The thief comes only in order to steal, kill, and destroy.*

**John 10:10**

# 1

## Gathering mentality

*I am the way, the truth, and the life; no one goes to the*
*Father except by me.*

**John 14:6**

Once upon a time, there was an outlaw who lived in the woods and was greatly appreciated by the poor and homeless because of his generosity. He stole whatever he could lay his hands on from the rich and famous and divided his spoil among the common folk, who thought he was a hero and endorsed his way of living. It so happened, that stealing became accepted as a way to survive and to get even with society. Of course, they all lived happily ever after.

Ah, childhood memories! Robin Hood's tale became famous all over the world. The audience just loved his adventurous spirit and rebellion against the establishment. He stood up for the poor and disabled; he wanted to change their destiny. What a story. I am recollecting his adventures, because he is probably the most admired and legendary thief in history and the book you are holding deals with thievery. Well, at least part of the book does, but there is more. This book not only deals with the way of the thief, which is *taking*, but also with the way of the Master, which is *giving*. In this book, I present two opposite ways of living, it is our choice that will make all the difference. We will soon find out that the way of the thief goes way beyond the hands in the cookie jar and Robin's legend, and that the way of the Master goes far beyond our coins in the offering tray and the hours of church volunteering. But let us start where it all begins, the eighth commandment.

The ancient biblical commandment simply says, 'Do not steal' and it can't really get any clearer than that, or so I thought. While studying the subject however, I learned there is much more to the eighth commandment than merely obeying such a rule. At the core, this commandment deals with the attitude of our hearts and the understanding of God's purpose behind these three simple words. As we have already seen in the previous books in this series, there is more to God's Word than just obeying a set of rules; it is about living it, fulfilling it, and applying it in our daily lives and in doing so advancing the kingdom of God.

I would like to invite you to open up your hearts for what the Bible wants to teach us about taking and giving. If you would rather not change the way you already think: put this book back on the shelf. The purpose is to shift your thought patterns according to the teachings of Jesus.

That might turn out to be an uncomfortable exercise, but it is worth the effort: your life will never be the same again! Please, set aside the thought that the Ten Commandments are old-fashioned rules that no one can live by. The purpose of this book is to find out what Jesus said about the eighth commandment and how He expects us to act upon it. I would like to challenge you to re-focus present day thinking towards His teachings. Often, our thinking about God's Word is rigid; many of us haven't adjusted pre-conceived ideas about the Bible since our high school days. It is time to dust the scriptures off!

The old teachings and sayings are still relevant and applicable today, but I believe it will surely help to upgrade the language a little. I have no doubt that 'thou shalt not steal' is a universally accepted rule, but I think it is time for some fresh insights on this ancient truth. The eighth commandment is more than a moral code because in it is hidden a philosophy that has the power to change a person's life. Jesus lifted the veil of this hidden secret when He had His encounter with the rich, young man, as we will see in the next chapter. I hope and pray that through this book you will see that the revolutionary teachings of Jesus are the source of life, a life in all its fullness. His life on earth turned out to be the fulfillment of everything said and written in the Old Testament, as the apostle Paul writes in 2 Corinthians 1:19-20,

*... he is God's "Yes"; for it is he who is the "Yes" to all of God's promises.*

I feel free to say that Jesus is the positive answer in an often-negative world. We can learn so much from Him.

For example, Jesus told His audience that the whole law and all teachings depended on only two things: loving God and loving others as yourself (Matthew 22:37-40). Most of us know that scripture all too well, but when asked to explain what that means in our daily life, we might hesitate to answer. I know that feeling. That is why I have taken a simple commandment like 'Do not steal' out of her birthplace in history and placed it right in the middle of our present day and age. We are very privileged to live in the age of the Holy Spirit because we have such a rich history to look back on and learn from:

- We can read in the Old Testament how God lead the people of that time.
- We can read in the gospels how Jesus lead the people of His time, and
- We can read in the epistles how the Holy Spirit leads the people of our time.

In John 14:26, not long before He left earth to be with God the Father, Jesus explained the need of the Spirit in everyone's life,

*The Helper, the Holy Spirit, whom the Father will send in my name, will teach you everything and make you remember all that I have told you.*

The Holy Spirit keeps the words of Jesus alive in us. We are able to tap into His teachings today and they will turn out to be as fresh as ever. We will therefore follow the Spirit's guidance and study the teaching of Jesus regarding the eighth commandment.

Exodus 20:15 says, 'Do not steal.' For most of us, this commandment is an easy one to understand and to live up to. Don't take anything without permission. Maybe you are thinking: 'I do not steal. I am not a thief. Why then should I read this book?' As we have seen in the previous books in this series, Jesus has a way of opening our eyes to the commandments. He turns them upside down and inside out.

When we say we don't steal, when we state we are not thieves, we are only being obedient to the Law. We are not fulfilling it. Obeying the Law to the letter is not the same as fulfilling it in love, and Romans 13:10 (NIV) says:

*Love is the fulfillment of the law.*

The coming of Jesus to earth did not end the Law, but it surely changed the purpose forever. For centuries, people had tried to become better men by obeying the Law, but the harder they tried, the more they failed. When Jesus came, He offered the solution to men's problem with sin when He took the sins of all mankind upon His shoulders on the cross. In doing so, He did not give us an excuse to ignore His commandments, on the contrary. He showed us that love is the fulfillment of the Law. Romans 8:3-4 describes it quite well,

*What the Law could not do, because human nature was weak, God did. He condemned sin in human nature by sending his own Son, who came with a nature like our sinful nature, to do away with sin. God did this so that the righteous demands of the Law might be fully satisfied in us who live according to the Spirit, and not according to human nature.*

Only through His grace and our faith in Jesus Christ can we be at peace with God. Good deeds or strict obedience will never ever bring us into relationship with God. So, because of Jesus, the emphasis on obeying the Law has moved to fulfilling the Law. He himself turned the Law into love by giving up His life for us when He was crucified. Jesus explains over and over again how to fulfill the words of His Father in love.

Regarding the eighth commandment, for example, He tells us what we should do instead of stealing. He wants to replace the desire to take for ourselves with a desire to give to others. He wants to change our thought patterns

as well as our behavioral patterns. He teaches us how to
redirect our focus, from taking to giving.

***Meditate on the following:***

- *Can I think of something in my life I'd rather receive than give?*
- *Love is the fulfillment of the law. How does that play out in my life?*

***Journal your thoughts:***

# 2

## *The great reversal*

*My children, our love should not be just words and talk;
it must be true love, which shows itself in action.*

**1 John 3:18**

Let us take a look at a familiar historical encounter Jesus had with a wealthy young man. You will find the story in Matthew 19:16-22 (MSG, emphasis mine)

*Another day, a man stopped Jesus and asked, Teacher, what good things must I do to get eternal life?*

*Jesus said, Why do you question me about what is good? God is the One who is good. If you want to enter the life of God, just do what he tells you.*

*The man asked, What in particular?*

*Jesus said, Don't murder, don't commit adultery, **don't steal**, don't lie, honor your father and mother, and love your neighbor as you do yourself.*

*The young man said, I've done all that. What's left?*

*<u>If you want to give it all you've got</u>, Jesus replied, go sell your possessions, **give** everything to the poor. All your wealth will be in heaven. Then come follow me."*

Now, we know that this man was very wealthy and he decided not to give up his lifestyle in order to follow Jesus, but that is not the part of the story we want to look into. In this short dialogue we can see the difference between serving God in the old way of the written law and serving in the new way of the Spirit, as explained in Romans 7:6.

The young man kept the commandments, but somehow it did not give him security, satisfaction, and fulfillment; that is why he decided to ask Jesus what else to do. At first Jesus replies the way the people of that time liked it: 'Just follow the Law; do this, don't do that. Don't steal.' The young man just feels in his gut there must be more and he keeps asking. That is when Jesus gives him the clue: 'Go, sell, and give…' In just a few words, He reverses the commandment. Not stealing translated into love is giving. The Message translation calls it the Great Reversal in Matthew 19:30. Jesus promises the young man treasures in Heaven and even qualifies him for discipleship if he is willing to live the way Jesus just explained to him, the way of the Master.

In this encounter Jesus teaches all of us an important lesson: in order to get full satisfaction, in order to enter the real life, we should become givers. Just saying 'I don't steal' is not enough to be called a follower of Jesus; He wants givers. He requires action, not passive obedience. In Matthew 5:17 the Lord explains His position in regard to the Law,

*Do not think that I have come to do away with the Law of Moses and the teachings of the prophets. I have not come to do away with them, but to make their teachings come true.*

Jesus is our example on how to make the old teachings come true. He requires action from us as well. By becoming givers, we fulfill the Law. We should no longer focus on what we shouldn't do, but on what we can do. If you still have the 'thou shalt nots' running through your brain, it is time to replace them with some 'I want to's.'

Think about the time you wanted to quit a bad habit; maybe it was smoking or eating sweets. It only made matters worse when your thought pattern was focused on the forbidden thing. Going around all day telling yourself I should not smoke. I should not smoke, amplified the problem and activated your craving (and probably drove you crazy). A well-known method for conquering bad habits is replacing them with good ones. It starts with talking to ourselves about good things. I am allowed to do this or that, I love to do this or that, etc.

Jesus used that method too. He did not go around all the time telling people 'do not steal, do not steal.' That would only have amplified their sin and shortcomings. Instead, He went around giving them advice on how to live a life pleasing to God. He even went as far as teaching them to love their enemies and that included the people that stole from them and to not ask for the stolen goods back. I know; that sounds too weird to be true, but read Luke 6:30 in the context.

*Give to everyone who asks you for something, and when someone takes what is yours, do not ask for it back.*

Now, that is revolutionary thinking, isn't it? He did not say, 'take them to court and sue them.' He said, 'love them and do good to them.' Do you see why we still have need for His teaching regarding the eighth commandment?

Jesus shows us how to live a life of giving instead of taking. As far as we know, we either have to buy, beg, borrow, or steal in order to get something. According to Jesus we have to give in order to get something. That doesn't make sense in this world, but it does in the kingdom of God. In Luke 6:38 we can read His wise words.

*Give to others, and God will give to you. Indeed, you will receive a full measure, a generous helping, poured into your hands—all that you can hold. The measure you use for others is the one that God will use for you.*

The Message translation says, 'Giving, not getting is the way. Generosity begets generosity.' We all want the full measure, the generous helping, but are we willing to do the same for others? If so, how do we start? How do we become cheerful givers and how can we replace the thief's mentality? How can we shift our all-too-human, attitude of getting into an attitude of giving?

We are so programmed to spend most of our lives accumulating things, which we think will make us happier and give us a more fulfilled life, whether it is the house, the car, the boat, the job, the money, or the mate we desire. The root of that gathering mentality is the way of the thief, and I hope you agree with me that that way is not going to make us happy.

Are you ready to fill your mind with new thoughts, your heart with new love and your spirit with fresh insights? I invite you to open up for the new way of the Spirit.

***Meditate on the following:***

- *Have I ever conquered a bad habit? If yes, how?*
- *No matter what my age or position, am I open to teaching?*

***Journal your thoughts:***

# 3

*Life in all its fulness*

*The Lord is my shepherd; I have everything I need.*

**Psalm 23:1**

When I first started my walk with the Lord, I didn't know much about giving. Each time a preacher would start on the subject I would squirm in my seat and only one thought occupied my mind, 'they're after my money.'

The mere mentioning of the word 'tithing' would bring shivers up and down my spine and I would debate each and every person who followed certain principles for giving, especially when they came from the Old Testament. The Sunday in October 2002, when my husband and I first set foot in the Solid Rock Christian Center in Ventura, California, the teaching was on 'How to Become a Hilarious Giver' and believe it or not, we became cheerful givers from that day on. The Lord transformed our minds completely.

I am using my own experience to illustrate how the power of the Holy Spirit can renew our thinking, even in one day. Sometimes we just need to hear a certain word or receive new revelation on a subject in order to review our thought patterns and often pre-conceived ideas. I have been trained to maintain a teachable spirit and I would like to ask you to do the same. Bear with me as we will walk through a very familiar scripture as the basis for our new way of looking at the eighth commandment. That scripture is John 10:10, and I am sure most of you are familiar with it.

*The thief comes only in order to steal, kill, and destroy. I have come in order that you might have life – life in all its fullness.*

It wouldn't surprise me if John 10:10, or at least part of it, turns out to be one of the most quoted scriptures. Within Christian circles we can hear it in churches, on television, and on the radio. We can read it in books and magazines, and we will find it on the internet. We just love the part where Jesus says that He came so that we might have life, life in all its fullness—also called the abundant life. I love that scripture too. It holds a wonderful promise, it speaks about Jesus' love for mankind, and it tells us something about the kind of life we should live as Christians.

I would like to take a look at verse ten as a whole as well as in the context of the parable of the good shepherd that precedes this statement. Jesus amplifies the purpose of His coming to earth (to bring life) because others who came before Him tried to deceive people by showing them the wrong track and thus taking (stealing) their lives. In verse eight Jesus calls them thieves and robbers. Therefore John 10:10 not only holds a promise for a life in all its fullness, but a warning as well. Jesus wants to teach us important insights regarding the choices we make every day, especially when it is about *taking* (with or without permission) and *giving.*

Verse ten is only a part of the speech Jesus gave to explain the parable of the good shepherd, as told at the beginning of John 10. Jesus states that He is to be compared with the gate and that everyone who comes in through that gate will be saved. He came to give life to everyone by saving mankind from a destructive and sinful nature that will eventually end in death. Entering life through the gate (Jesus' way) will bring us no ordinary life, but eternal bliss in His presence and a preceding life in all its fullness here on earth.  When Jesus promises life, a life in all its fullness, He is serious. He wants it for everyone. In verse nine, He says, *Whoever comes in by me will be saved.* We just love to hear that part of the abundant life, but do we ever ask ourselves if we are entering it His way?

For good reasons, Jesus warns us that there are also people who are trying to enter that abundant life through another door, using other ways. We are talking futile ways here, because they imply stealing, killing, and destroying. In other words, the ways of a thief. In John 10:1 Jesus says very clearly,

*I am telling you the truth: the man who does not enter the sheep pen by the gate, but climbs in some other way, is a thief and a robber.*

I had to read that verse over and over again. Somehow, it is possible to climb in some other way. Somehow, it is possible to sneak in without showing ourselves to the gatekeeper. Could it be true that we have been trying to enter a life in all its fullness via the back door? Maybe you find this a ridiculous question. Maybe you are saved, you got delivered from your hurts and hang-ups, you are born again, you know all about eternal life and you love God. You don't have to sneak in anywhere.

Let me ask you another question. Are you living a life in all its fullness? Are all your needs met? Are all areas in your life balanced? If you answer one of these questions with a 'no', this might be a good time to consider the words in John 10:10. When Jesus states He came to give us a life in all its fullness, He is not lying. He starts off in verse seven saying, 'I am telling you the truth'. So, if we are not experiencing that wonderful life, we have to check our own attitude, not His. Is it possible that we are trying to enter that abundant life as a thief? In the words of Luke 6:38, are we trying to receive the full measure, the generous helping, without giving to others? Serious questions, aren't they?

Now, don't get nervous or discouraged about this whole thing. As I stated in chapter one, the purpose of this book is to shift our thought pattern according to Jesus' teaching. He wants to teach us a lot more than not stealing. He desires to teach us giving.

John 10:10 contains the warning, the grace, and the promise. We will stay with this scripture and do the following:

- We will look into some ways of stealing that have become common practice in our society. We will check our attitudes and hopefully re-shape our actions in that field.
- We will look into the way Jesus came to bring life: by giving up His own! It is through His grace that we are able to change from gatherers into givers.
- We will look at life in all its fullness: balance in spirit, soul, and body.

***Meditate on the following:***

- *Which area of my life is out of balance? (Think spiritual, emotional, physical, financial etc.)*
- *Abundant life… try to describe what that would look like.*

***Journal your thoughts:***

# 4

## *My way or His way*

*We have not received this world's spirit; instead, we have received the Spirit sent by God, so that we may know all that God has given us.*

**1 Corinthians 2:12**

According to John 10:10 the thief comes in order to steal, kill, and destroy. That is a serious warning. Jesus is talking about the devil himself in this verse. After all, it was the devil who temporarily stole the perfect life of mankind in the Garden of Eden, and it was the devil who tried to steal Jesus' loyalty to God the Father when he tempted Him in the desert.

Although we do not like to think about it, the Bible is quite clear about the actions of the devil. In 1 Peter 5:8 we can read the following warning,

*Be alert, be on watch! Your enemy, the Devil, roams around like a roaring lion, looking for someone to devour.*

The devil's intentions are clear: he wants to deceive, destroy, and bring overall destruction. When Jesus refers to Satan in John 10:10, He simply specifies the thief's character. He does so in contrast with His own character, as we can read in the same verse when He comforts the reader with these words, 'I have come in order that you might have life.' Mentioning the thief's assignment is not just a simple statement, it is a serious warning. Jesus knows about the works of the thief, and He warns people not to follow his destructive ways, but instead to always follow the voice of the good shepherd. He says this because He knows the different end results. The thief takes life, Jesus gives life, and it is as simple as that. He repeated in a different way the words of His Father who spoke to the Israelites some 1400 years earlier. In Deuteronomy 30:19 God told them,

*I am now giving you the choice between life and death, between God's blessing and God's curse, and I call heaven and earth to witness the choice you make. Choose life.*

We have almost grown comfortable in blaming God for everything that goes wrong in this world, and we ask Him quite often why He allows certain things to happen. Sometimes we forget that God has given us a voice and a choice. The same choice He has set before the ancient Israelites still applies to all of us, every day. In John 10:9 Jesus tells us,

*I am the gate. Those who come in by me will be saved;
they will come in and go out and find pasture.*

The only way to enter a new life is through Jesus Christ
and we must purposely and consciously choose to go that
way. When we do so, it is His wonderful promise that we
will find pasture, in other words: we will find life!

His way brings life, the way of the thief brings death.
Now, you might be thinking, I know all this. I am
choosing life. I am a follower of Jesus. I can't go wrong.
Good, then you may have entered the life in all its
fullness, just the way Jesus promised. However, maybe
you are not sure if you are always choosing the right
thing to do. You desire to follow Jesus' way, but in
reality, quite often, you follow your own way. The
apostle Paul briefly explains such a struggle in Romans
8. It might be worthwhile to read this chapter from a
translation that speaks to you. Verses five and six teach
us the following:

*Those who live as their human nature tells them to, have
their minds controlled by what human nature wants.
Those who live as the Spirit tells them to, have their
minds controlled by what the Spirit wants.*

*To be controlled by human nature results in death; to be
controlled by the Spirit results in life and peace.*

Wow that must be what Jesus is talking about in John 10:10. His way brings life, life in all its fullness, and the thief's way brings death.

Now, the thief's way must be part of our human nature, if Paul is correct. I believe Jesus warns us about the ways of the thief  because He knows our weakness: we would rather take than give because we are selfish by nature. We would rather choose our own ways than God's ways. That is why He is offering us the help of His Holy Spirit. We would have a terrible time figuring this all out in our own power and strength. The Holy Spirit can show us the truth and convince us of certain principles in a few seconds time. I personally know this from experience, since He changed my attitude about giving just like that. In John 14:16-17 Jesus says,

*I will ask the Father, and he will give you another Helper, who will stay with you forever. He is the Spirit, who reveals the truth about God. The world cannot receive him, because it cannot see him or know him. But you know him, because he remains with you and is in you.*

In the next chapter, we will take a look at some ways of the thief that have slowly entered our lives (remember: the devil is a cunning deceiver) without us realizing it. I am not afraid to admit that I need the help of the Spirit every day.

Without a doubt. the most obvious form of stealing is taking someone else's stuff without permission. But did you know that we can steal someone's time too? And what about someone's joy, ideas, partner, or even someone's freedom? The purpose of this book is definitely not to accuse anyone of stealing. I want us all to think about our attitudes: do we treat someone else's possessions, time, or feelings with respect and care? Do we intrude in other people's business or family life? Do we collect for ourselves or do we share with others? Simple questions, but the answers will make all the difference in our life in all its fullness.

I would like to emphasize, like I did in the previous books, that my writings are about living a life in the way of the Spirit, they are not about keeping the Law. We have a commission to love God and one another and love is the fulfillment of the Law. Jesus says in John 14:15,

*If you love me, you will obey my commandments.*

Saying we love Jesus and going around saying we are Christians means nothing if we don't obey His teaching. He is always probing us to look at our own lives (not the lives of others, by the way) and work out the elements in our characters that are not yet Christ-like. That is not a burden; it is a wonderful journey through the seasons of our lives; a journey that will enhance our relationship with God. We do work on our human relationships, don't we? Why not take a serious look at Jesus' warning in John 10:10 and find out whether He is talking to us?

***Meditate on the following:***

- *Can I think of moments/situations when I follow my own ways?*
- *Would I call myself a giver or a gatherer? Be honest!*

***Journal your thoughts:***

# 5



*Time is precious*

*Teach us to number our days, that we may gain a heart of wisdom.*

**Psalm 90:12 (NIV)**

The most awesome part of Christianity is the sacrificial death and resurrection of Jesus Christ. He took the punishment for the sins of mankind and died a gruesome death on the cross. He rose from the grave and in doing so won victory over sin and death.

He did this so that we could be forgiven and thus be free from guilt, fear, and condemnation. He made it possible for us to live our life in all its fullness, starting here on earth. The forgiveness of our sins is pure grace; we didn't have to do anything to deserve it. However, we are expected to turn away from our sinful lifestyles. Yeah, that is what true repentance means, leaving our old ways behind and embracing God's ways. Jesus tells us to stop sinning (Matthew 18:6-9, Luke 13:5, John 8:11) and to forgive others who sin (Matthew 6:15). It wouldn't hurt therefore, to check our behavior every now and then to see if we are living up to His commands. Sometimes we get so caught up in our daily routines, we don't even think about all of our actions anymore. We live parts of our lives on automatic pilot and because we live in a world polluted by sin, it is easy to become entangled in ungodly practices without even realizing it. The apostle Paul warns us in Romans 12:2 (AMP) with the familiar words,

*And do not be conformed to this world [any longer with its superficial values and customs], but be transformed and progressively changed [as you mature spiritually] by the renewing of your mind [focusing on godly values and ethical attitudes], so that you may prove [for yourselves] what the will of God is, that which is good and acceptable and perfect [in His plan and purpose for you].*

Do not be conformed any longer… that indicates we used to be conformed to the pattern of the world, maybe even without knowing it. Let's take a closer look at the ways of the thief and find out if action is necessary in any area of our lives.

## Stealing Stuff

This is the most obvious form of stealing; taking someone else's possessions without permission, whether from a store, a house, a car, or a company. Now, most of us probably don't go around stealing things from the store or breaking into people's houses to run off with expensive electronic devices. There is a chance, however, that we do steal from our employers without even thinking about it. I have worked as a temporary employee in many different companies for more than twenty years and I have seen office supplies, printing paper, building materials, and even flat computer screens disappear overnight.

Now, there is a difference between a computer screen and a fluorescent marker; but the root of the problem is the same: without asking, we are taking something home we haven't paid for. What about making a few private copies on the corporate machine during lunch breaks? We figure it is sort of okay because we are employees, we might even think we have a right to access the resources our boss provides us with. The common excuse is: 'Everyone is doing it!' In the process, we keep adjusting our limits. We say, 'No one misses a pen or a folder. No one misses a box of pens or a stack of folders.'

The Bible does not use the terms employer and employee that much; it uses the terms master and slave, which are more appropriate for that time. The relational principles, however, are still the same. With that in mind, see if you can relate to the way work relations are being described in Titus 2:9-10,

*Slaves are to submit themselves to their masters and please them in all things. They must not talk back to them*

*or steal from them. Instead, they must show that they are always good and faithful, so as to bring credit to the teaching about God our Savior in all they do.*

Quite clear, isn't it? Why not ask for permission to take something home for personal use? Why not be honest, even about the small stuff? Please, don't forget; if you are known as a Christian at work, you will be watched. All the time! As we can see in the above-mentioned scripture, we must show that we are good and faithful, and in doing so we will be living testimonies wherever we go, that includes the work place.

## Stealing Time

Today, millions of people are using internet, wifi, and smartphones during work hours to retrieve e-mails, send letters, check the stock market, order books, catch up on social media and whatever other interesting things might be accessible. Quite often, personal phone and internet use at work starts with fifteen minutes during lunch break and slowly extends when the boss isn't looking or comes in late. Hours and hours of precious time are wasted every day by employees sitting behind computer and phone screens, doing things they are not supposed to do at work. Let me say boldly (and I am talking to myself here too!): we are stealing time from our employers. Not just time, but money too, since we're getting paid while doing it. We are using hours for ourselves that are reserved for the company.

You might be thinking I am taking this way too seriously, but imagine what is going on in a country as big as the USA for example. We are probably talking millions of hours every day here. Personally, I have learned that it is useful, for my own protection, to check on internet use regularly, at work and at home. How much time am I spending on the internet? Am I wasting time on the internet? Am I trying to hide things when the boss comes in? Is everything I watch useful? The Bible gives advice in Colossians 3:22-23,

*Slaves, obey your human masters in all things, not only when they are watching you because you want to gain their approval; but do it with a sincere heart because of your reverence for the Lord. Whatever you do, work at it with all your heart, as though you were working for the Lord and not for people.*

Stealing time happens in various ways in the corporate world. I remember when I first started working as a temporary employee in the USA. Pretty soon, I noticed that my co-workers would go on a lunch break, come back two hours later *with* their lunch in a paper bag, and eat it in front of all the others! The smell of French fries or burritos would linger in the office all afternoon. I was baffled by this whole thing. If the lunch break wasn't for lunch, what was it for? After a while, I didn't think anything of it anymore. I guess I slowly got used to the idea. I am bringing this up as an example to show you how easy it is to adapt behavior that in its deepest core is wrong. We adapt, simply because everyone is doing it. I don't think it would do us harm to check our own attitudes regarding these things. I believe that if we want to walk the way of Jesus we should say no to the way of the thief. Proverbs 20:6 says,

*Everyone talks about how loyal and faithful he is, but just try to find someone who really is!*

It is possible to steal precious time from family and friends too, just by talking endlessly on the phone. Praise God for modern communication. Email, telephone, internet, it is all wonderful as long as we don't abuse it. I just love to talk to my family members overseas, and we give each other updates on our work, the weather, the upcoming vacation, etc.

My husband and I travel all over the globe and stay in touch with loved ones by phone and internet. We can really cheer people up by sending them a card or by giving them a call and a kind word. I hope it is clear that I am not talking about that here. I am talking about useless chatter, complaining, or gossiping over the phone without realizing that the other person might be right in the middle of work or on the way to do something else.

I have met people who always complain about not having enough time to get everything done and organized; but when I see them, they are always talking on or looking at their phone. If you, even vaguely, have the feeling you spend too much time talking on the phone or chatting on the computer, try to think ahead of what you want to share or ask and be determined to keep it short. I believe that by the unrestricted use of phones and internet we are stealing precious time from the twenty-four hours that were given to us that day (let's face it: we could do a million other things in the same time) and we are also stealing time from the person we are talking to.

I have seen teenagers failing a year in school as the result of too much chatter on their phones or behind their game consoles. They stole a whole year of precious education time from themselves. Games can be fun, phone and computer conversations can be wonderful, but let's try to keep them short. Simply tell your friends and family members that time is precious to you and that you like to keep your phone conversations short and your bills low. Proverbs 10:19 warns us,

*The more you talk, the more likely you are to sin. If you are wise, you will keep quiet.*

Well, with all the noise and endless talk around us nowadays, wisdom has become scarce, for sure.

Let me finish this chapter with a word of wisdom from Ecclesiastes 3:7 (NIV) where it says that there is a time for everything,

*A time to be silent and a time to speak.*

Silence is never a waste of time!

*Meditate on the following:*

- *Do I do things just because everyone is doing it?*
- *Do I see myself as honest and faithful?*

*Journal your thoughts:*

# 6

*Say 'no' to the thief!*

*Be generous, and you will be prosperous. Help others, and you will be helped.*

**Proverbs 11:25**

Stealing stuff and stealing time. I never realized that could come so close. Let's continue for a little bit more and take a closer look at the ways of the thief and find out if action is necessary in any area of our lives.

**Stealing Joy**

Do you recognize the following situation? You wake up in the morning in a good mood; the day ahead looks wonderful. You like your looks in the mirror; you have money in your pocket and some time to spare later in the afternoon for a walk on the beach. All in all, it is going to be a wonderful day. You check in at work, enjoy your hot coffee, and start working. Somehow, an hour or so later, you start wondering what has come over you. You feel irritated, you don't like your job, and it feels like this is the longest day of your life. What in the world happened? Where did your joy go?

If this sounds like a familiar situation to you, you have experienced how it feels when someone steals your joy. Someone sucked the life out of you. Maybe you didn't even notice, but it happened anyway. It happened to the Galatians. The Apostle Paul hardly recognizes the people when he visits them again, 'You were so happy, what has happened?' The NIV translation says, 'What has happened to all your joy?' (They lost their joy because of legalism, by the way.) So, we should regularly ask ourselves: 'Do I guard my joy or am I one of those who always try to bring others down, simply because I can't stand their optimism?'

In my first book Sacred Sabbath, I wrote a whole chapter on joy and called it divine happiness. According to Nehemiah 8:10 the joy of the Lord is our strength. If we lose our joy, we will lose our strength. We will be like Samson without hair! When attacked, we will lose; we will be like a fighter without armor, defenseless. On the other hand, if we steal joy from others, by talking negative, for example, we will weaken them.

We are supposed to encourage one another and build each other up, as stated in 1 Thessalonians 5:11, not talk each other down. Verse 16 of the same chapters says, 'Be joyful, always!' As Christians, we have a calling to be joyful. Wherever we appear on the scene, the atmosphere should go up.

## Stealing from God

The book of Malachi holds an oracle, which is a divine announcement, of God. Read part of it as written in Malachi 3:8-10 (NIV):

*"Will a mere mortal rob God? Yet you rob me.*

*"But you ask, 'How are we robbing you?'*

*"In tithes and offerings. You are under a curse—your whole nation—because you are robbing me. Bring the whole tithe into the storehouse, that there may be food in my house. Test me in this," says the Lord Almighty, "and see if I will not throw open the floodgates of heaven and pour out so much blessing that there will not be room enough to store it.*

God is talking about the tithe here, the tenth of our income that belongs to Him. Somehow, people were not bringing the whole tithe to the temple. In our modern-day time, that would be the same as saying you give Him your tithes but in reality are only giving four percent of your income, for example. That is not tithing. Tithing is giving God ten percent of everything that comes in.

Tithing is just the training wheels for generous giving as taught to the New Testament believers. The most interesting part about His oracle in Malachi 3 is verse 6 (NIV),

*I, the Lord do not change.*

God speaks the same words to us as He spoke to the Israelites. He hasn't changed His mind. He does not want us to steal from Him or others, and He still wants to bless us beyond our imagination if we obey.

The previous examples are just that, examples. There are numerous ways to steal something, most likely without realizing it. It is possible to steal ideas or business concepts. It is possible to steal someone's dignity through manipulation or physical abuse. It is possible to steal a nation's or people's freedom through political pressure or torture. What about tax evasion? What about stealing someone's partner by having an affair? And so on, and so on. Stealing is more than taking the cookie out of the jar. Stealing has its roots in wanting more, more, and more. It is the way of the thief, a wicked way that will lead to destruction. That is why Jesus put out that serious warning in John 10:10, the thief comes only to steal, kill, and destroy. We must say no to the ways of the thief!

It is the enemy's assignment to numb our senses to the fact that we are being dishonest or greedy. He wants to push his vile character on us. Thank God for the second part of that verse where Jesus presents a higher plan for mankind: a better life as a result of His abundant grace!

***Meditate on the following:***

- *How do I give to God? How do I see tithing?*
- *In what areas in my life can I become a giver?*

***Journal your thoughts:***

**Pray aloud:**

*Dear Father in heaven, thank You for Your Word. I can still learn from it today. Thank you for opening my eyes to Your teachings. I want to be challenged. I realize You want me to have a real life, a life in all its fullness.*

*Holy Spirit, help me to change my ways and to renew my mind. I want to be excited about the Truth. No longer do I want to give room to the deceiving ways of the thief; I want to follow Your instructions. From now on I want to be controlled by the Spirit, because I know that will lead to life!*

*In the name of Jesus, I ask this. Amen.*

# Part II

# The Grace

*I have come in order that you might have life.*

**John 10:10**

# 7

---

## *Abundant grace*

*He saved us and called us to be his own people, not because of what we have done, but because of his own purpose and grace.*

**2 Timothy 1:9**

In the previous chapters, we have looked at the warning Jesus gave regarding the ways of the thief. We checked certain areas in our lives to see if we are still controlled, somehow, by the thief's deceiving ways. *It is okay to do it, everyone is doing it,* and *it won't harm me,* are in reality very quiet whispers of the enemy. His goal is to take our lives. His goal is to keep us from entering a life in all its fullness.

Jesus' goal, however, is to give us that life. The first and most important action Jesus took towards giving us that life was giving His own life. In John 10:11 He says,

*I am the good shepherd, who is willing to die for the sheep.* [He explains further in verse 17] *The Father loves me because I am willing to give up my life, in order that I may receive it back again.*

Jesus understood the kingdom principle of giving in order to receive. He practiced it in the most radical and ultimate way. He gave His life for others in order to receive it back from God. That sounds weird, but it is a principle we can see throughout the Bible; give and it shall be given to you. Giving is always tied to a blessing and that is why it is so much better than stealing.

Jesus taught this principle to the people of His time who couldn't really grasp the concept of letting go of things in order to receive them back. Well, aren't we struggling to accept the same teaching today? In Luke 6:38 Jesus says:

*Give to others and God will give to you. Indeed, you will receive a full measure, a generous helping, poured into your hands – all that you can hold.*

He knew everyone wanted to be on the receiving end, but not many wanted to be givers. He knew people would always be crying out for more, always asking, and always finding ways to accumulate, so He set His own life as an example. Jesus was (and is) a giver. He gave us His love in order that He would receive our love in return! Giving is loving; loving is giving. 1 John 3:16 says,

*This is how we know what love is: Christ gave his life for us. We too, then, ought to give our lives for others!*

Wow. Jesus is indeed our ultimate example. He has the opposite nature of the thief, who always wants to take and who is controlled by his storage mentality. Jesus gives away freely and abundantly; He gave it all. He gave it all to us because He wants us to follow in His footsteps. He wants us to become givers as well.

According to Luke 6:38, only givers can receive abundantly from God. We can pray, plead, cry, and scream for God to bless us lavishly, but it is not going to happen until we give to others. Our giving sets the measure for His blessings for our own lives, according to Jesus's words in this passage; it is up to us how much we will receive. The measuring stick is in our hands, so to speak. In the last part of Luke 6:38 Jesus adds,

*The measure you use for others is the one that God will use for you!*

I am not making this up; Jesus says it. Do we truly believe God will bless us with enormous increase if we sparingly give Him our tithes and not a penny more, if we never joyfully give Him a thank offering, and if we keep throwing our small change in the offering box? Many people ask God for cars and houses, yet they are not willing to offer more than a few dollars, the price of a double latte, when an opportunity is given.

What do we expect when we use a very tight measure? God's Word is plain and simple when it comes to giving and receiving. Jesus's attitude was: I want you all, so I give it all.  He used the right measure: His life.

Now God is an absolutely awesome God because He shares whatever He has with us. Read the following Scriptures aloud and just tell yourself what you will receive from God, if you give Him your life:

*I will be given eternal life* (John 10:28)

*I will be given the keys of the Kingdom of heaven* (Matthew 16:19)

*I will be given authority over the evil spirits* (Mark 6:7)

*I will be given the knowledge of the secrets of the Kingdom of God* (Luke 8:9)

*I will be given the Holy Spirit when I ask Him* (Luke 11:13)

*I will be given the right to become God's child* (John 1:12)

*In my union with Christ, He will bless me by giving me every spiritual blessing in the heavenly world* (Ephesians 1:3)

I could probably fill this whole book with all the things God gives us through Jesus. If we have been given so much (everything we possibly need) why is it that we keep asking for more?

Listen to most of the prayers we offer. Notice our attitude in church and concentrate on the questions in a prayer group. 'God, will you…, God, bless me…, God, please give us…' and so we go on and on. Many times, we even ask for things God has already given us. We don't even know what we own. We have gathered so much spiritual stuff that we keep asking for things we already received.

God answers my prayer requests often with a scripture that pops up in my mind. The conversation goes somewhat like this:

Me: *God, please give me patience*

Holy Spirit: *but the fruit of the Spirit is ... patience* (Galatians 5:22 NIV)

Me: *God, please give me peace over this situation*

Holy Spirit: *it is my own peace that I give you* (John 14:27)

Me: *God, please give me wisdom.*

Holy Spirit: *But God has brought you into union with Christ Jesus, and God has made Christ to be our wisdom* (1 Corinthians 1:30)

Me: *God, bless me*

Holy Spirit: *For in union with Christ you have become rich in all things, including all speech and all knowledge* (1 Corinthians 1:5)

Whatever I ask for, God often answers through His Word. As a result of this, I can re-phrase my requests. My prayer becomes, 'God, please help me to use the patience You have given me. I need to practice.' And oh yes, will God give me situations in which to practice.

***Meditate on the following:***

- *What gifts, talents, blessings, and precious people has God given me?*
- *How am I using God's gifts and blessings?*

***Journal your thoughts:***

# 8

## *More, more, more*

*The group of believers was one in mind and heart. None of them said that any of their belongings were their own, but they all shared with one another everything they had.*

**Acts 4:32**

We have to ask ourselves a very serious question: if we have been given so much, why do we keep on asking for more? In our churches we are screaming, yelling, and hollering at God to bless us. We often seem to think the louder the better.

But you know what? I believe we are already blessed as the body of Christ. Read 1 Corinthians 1:5 again. Read it aloud. Read it five times! Make it personal, fill in your own name, fill in your church's name, and scream it from the rooftops,

*For in union with Christ you have become rich in all things, including all speech and all knowledge.*

We have been given it all. Now is the time to use it. We no longer have any business with the thief; we don't need to gather more, ask for more, or simply get more. We have been given it all. We have been storing up, and we just keep on asking for more. Aren't we doing the same as Adam and Eve did? They had everything they possibly needed and wanted: peace with God, a beautiful place to live, no crazy in-laws, and dominion over the earth. They had a perfect life. Yet, they wanted more. They were not givers; they took. They fell for the ways of the thief. That same mentality is our human nature. We always want more, even if we have enough.

One day I was driving down the 405 freeway in Southern California and I saw a billboard that said in big letters: 'It is always more, more, more with you Californians'. It was an ad for a certain car with a ridiculous amount of horsepower. Of course, this ad doesn't just speak to the folks on the West Coast; it speaks to all of us. When are we going to stop asking for more? We just love to buy, collect, store, possess, take, keep, and treasure.

I once had a part time job at one of those Self Storage places for a while. Self Storage has been a booming business in America for the last several decades or so. They popped up like mushrooms all over the country. The concept intrigued me. What do people need those cubicles for? One day I decided to ask the manager. He told me people store stuff in those places and pay for it. 'What kind of stuff?' I asked curiously. His answer left me speechless: 'Oh, just stuff they don't need.' I must have looked rather dumb with my mouth open and a big question mark above my head. People actually pay someone to keep stuff they don't need?! It blew me away. What about the garage? Can't they store in the garage? Well, everyone knows the answer to that, I presume. The garage is for the car. Needless to say, that most cars end up in the driveway because the garage is full of stuff that no one needs. However, it is one notch up from the stuff we probably never need again. I am not trying to be funny. I am using this analogy because it also applies to our spiritual lives.

We store up so much insight, so many teachings, so much knowledge, so many revelations, and whatever we can get in our notebooks while running from church to conference to Bible study to retreat sessions that we forget what we have in storage. When we need something, we don't go out looking through our stuff (too much work); we just go out and buy something new. We keep accumulating without really using what we have, without tapping into the resources we already possess. That mentality is the way of the thief: more, more, more.

Maybe you feel I am taking this too far, but listen to what Psalm 73:12 says,

*That is what the wicked are like. They have plenty and are always getting more.*

Always wanting more is a wicked way; it does not please God.

In order to become true givers, we have to let go of our gathering attitude. I believe we need to get rid of our storage mentality.   According to Jesus's words in Matthew 19:21, we should exchange our earthly possessions for true wealth in heaven. Looking back at part I of this book we have to ask ourselves again, would we rather take than give? Do we store up treasures or hand out treasures?

Now don't get mad at me because it sounds like I am endorsing the selling of our possessions (that was Jesus, by the way). I didn't say that; I just want us to check our inventory. Maybe we can find out why we gather, why we collect, and why we hang on to things we probably will never use again. Being a giver is not just dropping some money in the bucket at church. It is a lifestyle! It means not being attached to time, money, and possessions, but merely enjoying them. It means being able to give when there is a need, not just when it suits us.

Looking at our natural circumstances can be a great help in understanding our spiritual status. Are you living in a house full of stuff? Are your drawers chaotic? Is your garage a private warehouse? Do you pay for self-storage? Are you a collector? If you answer yes to one or more of these questions, then try to be honest while looking into your spiritual life. Do you truly seek to use the gifts God has given you? Or do you always ask for more? Have you honestly tried to tap into the endless resources God has put in you when you received your new spiritual life?

Jesus was and is a giver. His message was and is: give and it will be given to you. He warns us about the storage mentality in Matthew 6:19,

*Do not store up riches for yourselves here on earth, where moths and rust destroy, and robbers break in and steal.*

***Meditate on the following:***

- *What can be cleaned out of my garage/storage? Am I willing to let go of things I do not use?*
- *How can I bless others with my stuff?*

***Journal your thoughts:***

# 9

*Everything belongs to God*

*Don't worry about missing out. You'll find all your
everyday human concerns will be met.*

**Matthew 6:33 (MSG)**

We have become rich in all things in our union with
Christ (1 Corinthians 1:5). That is a truth we really need
to understand and accept. It shows God's character. He is
a giver; He gave his Son, who gave us life.

If God gave us so much, why do we sometimes hesitate
when it comes to giving something back? The Message
says in 2 Corinthians 8:9,

*You are familiar with the generosity of our Master, Jesus
Christ. Rich as he was, he gave it all away for us - in one
stroke, he became poor and we became rich.*

If we are so rich, if God has given us so much, how come
we still have the feeling God asks us to give from our
own resources? How come we count the cost when we
donate, share, pledge, or give? Are we afraid we will run
out of possessions or money? Are we afraid that we will

miss out on the blessings God is going to pour out? Of course, I realize we need to be good stewards when it comes to handling our money, and a good budget plan can really save us a bunch of trouble. But I dare to say that most of our offerings are more restricted and calculated than our expenses at the mall, at the golf course, and online. Spending money is easy and fun, until it comes to offering; suddenly we become very serious and reserved. Somehow, we see everything we own as ours, and every time we give away something, whether it is time, money, or possessions, we say good-bye to part of ourselves.

In reality, nothing is really ours; everything has been given to us to use while here on earth. God had to explain that to the Israelites in Leviticus 25:23,

*Your land must not be sold on a permanent basis, because you do not own it; it belongs to God, and you are like foreigners who are allowed to make use of it.*

God had given the Israelites everything they needed, and they started treating things as if they were their own. God declares His ownership over everything many times throughout the Bible. For example in Deuteronomy 10:14 (NIV),

*To the Lord your God belong the heavens, even the highest heavens, the earth, and everything in it.*

Please, let there be no misunderstanding about that. Throughout the ages, people may have been treating stuff, time, and money as their own, but in reality, everything belongs to the Lord.

According to 1 Timothy 6:17, He richly provides us with everything for our enjoyment. We may feel we have the right to call a couple of things our own, especially if we worked hard to get it, but we are only fooling ourselves. We actually limit ourselves when we call certain things our own. Sharing God's endless resources will make us the richest people on earth. Calling things our own could make us possessive and maybe even a little greedy. Sharing earth and heaven's riches with God and others will make us generous, since it is an endless resource.

I believe that in America, most people have a charitable spirit; we give to goodwill, we support the homeless, we organize food drives, and we drop our dollars in the solicitor's bucket at K-mart. We give because we have more than enough; we give because we are a blessed nation. In the western world, we are able to give offerings from our abundance (which is truly wonderful), and it hardly ever puts us in difficult situations. Let's face it: most of the time we give away what we don't need anymore (yes, the stuff that is not even worth the storage rent) or the money we can spare. We calculate our giving.

Now, Jesus has something else in mind; He talks about revolutionary giving. We have seen this when He talked with the rich guy in Matthew 19:21 where He advises him to sell his possessions and give to the poor. Jesus does not talk about calculated donations that are tax deductible, He explains giving the way He likes it: free, generous, and happy. He teaches us again about true giving (not the amount, but the attitude is what counts) in Luke 21:3-4 when He says,

*I tell you that this poor widow put in more than all the others. For the others offered their gifts from what they had to spare of their riches; but she, poor as she is, gave all she had to live on.*

This encounter shows us that we have to stop looking at things from a worldly point of view. A hundred-dollar bill is worth more than a one-dollar bill according to our way of thinking. According to Jesus's way of thinking one dollar is worth more than a hundred when it is all you've got. The amount of our giving doesn't matter to God (remember: He owns everything anyway), it is the attitude that counts.

It is easy to be a happy giver as long as we have more than enough for ourselves, but being a giver when we fear lack is much harder. Many of us have worked hard to gather the things we own: our house, furniture, appliances, clothes, a car or two, etc. It is one thing to give away some of the stuff we don't need anymore, but how about giving away stuff we don't want to let go of? It is easy to give when we can replace the goods with something new or better. That is why garage and yard sales bring some relief: by selling our stuff, we get some money in return which will supply us with new things. We somehow feel that everything we give away or sell to others needs to be replaced with something newer, better, or bigger. Since we feel we give away from our own resources, we also feel the need to replace and add new things to keep the balance. Sometimes we do not even give because we want to have less, we give because we need room for something else.

This is where we have to shift our thinking according to Jesus's teaching. We have to stop regarding everything as our stuff, our time, our money, and our things. When we reach the point where we are able to honestly believe that everything belongs to the Lord, and that He will supply whatever we need, we can give away freely, just like Jesus advises the young man in Matthew 19:21. When we reach the point where we truly understand and realize that we have been given everything (the whole kingdom) and that we have access to a never-ending supply of blessings and gifts, we can give away freely.

We no longer need to worry about replacing things, because God will take care of that! Every time He sees us giving, He will remember His promise to us, as mentioned in Luke 6:38.

*Give and it will be given to you!*

The flow will never stop. It only stops when we stop giving.

***Meditate on the following:***

- *Am I possessive?*
- *Do I truly believe that God will provide all my needs?*

***Journal your thoughts:***

# 10



## *Turning the key*

*Even strong young lions sometimes go hungry, but those who trust in the Lord will lack no good thing.*

**Psalm 34:10 (NLT)**

Maybe you are thinking right now, okay, if I give, God will make sure He will give to me and I do not have to worry about lacking anything, but somehow I still feel like I am giving part of myself away. The money I worked so hard for, the time that is so precious to me, the stuff I paid a lot of money for: how do I get rid of that possessiveness? How can I freely let go of what I have?

There is an absolutely awesome verse in 2 Corinthians 9:10:11. Please take note of this.

*And God, who supplies seed for the sower and bread to eat, will also supply you with all the seed you need and will make it grow and produce a rich harvest from your generosity. He will always make you rich enough to be generous at all times, so that many will thank God for your gifts which they receive from us.*

God is the one who supplies the seed we sow. Read that Scripture again. It doesn't say 'God, who supplies seed for the Christian, or the good people, or the Americans.' It says God will supply seed for the sower. For the one who is willing to give it away. It is not ours. He gives it to us to give away, and He promises to always make us rich enough to be generous at all times. God gives so we can be givers! Does that seem illogical to you? Maybe a metaphor, that my pastor in Ventura taught me, will help.

Imagine someone gives you an apple. You thank him for it. You eat the apple, enjoy the taste, and get strengthened by its vitamins. What happened here is that you received a seed, but you didn't give it a chance to grow and reproduce. You could have planted the apple in good soil, waited for a tree to come up, and then had hundreds of apples to eat and give away.

This principle is at work every day in our lives. We receive all kinds of things from God, whether it is time, money, health, goods, or talents. Remember what we read before: everything belongs to God. He gives it as a seed for us to sow and He will produce a rich harvest for us. It is up to us if we follow the way of the thief (wanting more, more, more for ourselves or, in other words, eating the apple) or the ways of Jesus (giving away freely or, in other words, planting the seed). This is not a chance we take; this is not gambling. We already know the outcome of our action. The way of the thief will bring destruction; the way of Jesus will bring life, a life in all its fullness!

Sometimes we worry so much about our giving. I could use the money for something else. I have bills to pay this week. I need that time for myself. How will my gift be used? We have to change our attitude; otherwise, we will still worry about the same things twenty years from now.

When my husband and I started our walk with the Lord, our thought pattern was still like that. Until the day my husband and I literally said to the Lord, "All we have is yours. Please teach us and show us how to handle it and how to be good caretakers." I remember we prayed over our money, ATM cards, checkbook, and wallets, and we dedicated them all to God. One day I received a phone call from a man who claimed to have found my husband's wallet (we had not missed it yet) with our phone number inside. I was happy for such an honest person, and my husband went immediately to the man's house to retrieve his wallet.

Upon arriving at the house, something strange happened: the man confessed that he didn't find the wallet; he had stolen it. He explained how he started hearing a very loud voice in his head saying, "Give it back! Give it back!" It became so intimidating that he could no longer keep the wallet in his house. He hid it in the garden, but the voice kept bothering him until he picked up the phone to call us. My husband was so moved by the confession that he gave the man the money in the wallet anyway and told him not to steal again!

Back home we rejoiced over the whole thing; we just knew God was in control. We knew we could trust Him with 'our' money! I truly believe that has been a turning point in our possessive attitude. God will indeed provide us with everything we possibly need, as long as we concentrate on His kingdom first. We didn't have to ask for our stolen goods back (Luke 6:30); the thief presented himself to us, and at that moment his encounter with God was much more important than the money. God used the money He had trusted us with to bring this man to repentance. What a wonderful concept.

Becoming givers and leaving the way of the thief behind seems difficult. It requires a change in attitude and, maybe even more so, a change of mind. We have to learn to focus on all the riches God shares with us and to no longer focus on our fear of lack. We have to learn to literally trust God with our time, stuff, and money and to stop telling Him what our calculations are. He wants to measure our level of obedience, not our bank account. We have to stop regarding everything as our possessions. Mine, mine, mine slowly becomes more, more, more. We must decide to leave the way of the thief behind.

We can start by concentrating on the fact that whatever we give, was God's already; that way giving becomes so much easier. David quite frankly speaks about this to God in 1 Chronicles 29:14 when he says,

*Yet my people and I cannot really give you anything, because everything is a gift from you, and we have only given back what is yours already.*

Becoming a true giver might seem as difficult for believers under the New Covenant as the commandment not to steal was for the people under the Old Covenant. However, we have the example of Jesus, the help of the Holy Spirit, and the grace of God.

Becoming a true giver turns out to be easy when we understand what those three can do for us. Once the light goes on, once we decide to turn the key, we will be on our way to a life in all its fullness!

***Meditate on the following:***

- *What are my biggest worries in every-day life?*
- *Am I willing to dedicate my money and possessions to the Lord?*

***Journal your thoughts:***

# 11

*Grace of giving*

*I tell you, now is the time of God's favor.*

**2 Corinthians 6:2 (NIV)**

It is one thing to leave behind the way of the thief and another thing to become a true giver; to follow in Jesus's footsteps and give it all you've got. It is one thing to say, 'I do not steal' but another thing to say, 'I am a giver.' How can giving become a desire of our hearts? How can giving become part of our new nature?

Let me ask you the following question: how can a sinner become righteous in God's eyes? How can we, as human beings, share in God's glory? One simple answer: grace. It is God's grace that makes many things possible for mankind. Grace is a word that we don't hear much outside the church, yet it is so powerful. Favor, mercy, or goodwill are more commonly used. The Penguin English Dictionary  describes grace as follows: 'supernatural power given by God to the soul to enable it to attain virtue and salvation'.

Grace is another one of God's gifts to us. Grace is God's free favor on our lives; we did not do anything to deserve it. When we receive that gift, we can start using it to overcome difficult situations. The dictionary says it is a supernatural power. The Bible explains more extensively what grace is and what it can do in our lives.

Jesus, for example, had God's grace on his life. Luke 2:40 (NIV) talks about Jesus's childhood:

*And the child grew and became strong; he was filled with wisdom, and the grace of God was on him.*

Grace was on him, that tells me grace is something extra, almost like a gift from God. God's grace was upon Jesus when He was a child. While growing older, the grace of God was no longer just upon Him, but it filled Him. That tells me Jesus grew in grace; He became full of it! The opening chapter of John's gospel contains the following statement, in verse 14,

*The Word became a human being and, full of grace and truth, lived among us.*

Now, God did not just reserve His grace for Jesus; He gave it also in abundance to the believers, beginning with the first disciples. Acts 4:33 (NIV) tells us that "much grace was upon them all" in the same way as it was in the beginning upon Jesus. However, the disciples grew in grace too. A couple of chapters later (Acts 6:8 NIV) the martyr Stephen for example is introduced as follows,

*Now Stephen, a man full of God's grace and power, did great wonders and miraculous signs among the people.*

Grace was not just upon him, but it filled him. Grace is so much more than a simple gift or a blessing; it is a power. God's grace does not stop at our salvation; we can continue to live in it and grow in it. Once we become conscious of His grace, His undeserved favor in our lives, we will find out that it will help us conquer and control many difficult situations.

As human beings, we have a tendency to depend on our own strength, to fight our battles all alone. We don't have to do that, because God's grace is there to sustain us. We need to learn to be aware of His grace in our life, which will save us a lot of trouble because it is not a one-time moment of truth, it is an ongoing experience in our lives. The apostle Paul knew that as no other. He opens the fifth chapter of the Book of Romans with the following words:

*Now that we have been put right with God through faith, we have peace with God through our Lord Jesus Christ. He has brought us by faith into this experience of God's grace, in which we now live.*

Paul simply states that by faith we can live in God's grace; he calls it an experience. Living in God's grace is something that will manifest itself in our lives for others to see. God's grace is a power that will back up the work we do, it will keep us from failing. Grace does not mean that we can rest on our lazy behinds and let God do all the work.

Praying, "God, make me a giver," without taking any action is not going to change anything. God's grace will help us to become givers when we start working on it. The apostle Paul must have experienced this quite clearly in his own life, because he describes the process in a few sentences and well in 1 Corinthians 15:10:

*But by God's grace I am what I am, and the grace that he gave me was not without effect. On the contrary, I have worked harder than any of the other apostles, although it was not really my own doing, but God's grace working with me.*

God's grace is working with him. That is the key to success. If we stop fighting our battles and struggling all alone, and we accept God's grace then it will work with us. We need to team up. Success is guaranteed.

From a human point of view, it is almost impossible to become a true giver in God's kingdom; we have to let go of so many sacred cows. With the help of God's grace, however, we are able to do this. It truly helps to no longer look at God's commandments as outward rules but rather as inward change. With the help of the Holy Spirit, it is possible to change our perspective and attitude from "thou shall not steal," to "I want to give." John 1:17 makes it clear:

*God gave the Law through Moses, but grace and truth came through Jesus Christ.*

Trying to work this out without accepting the grace that Jesus freely offers us is futile. It just won't work. With God's grace, however, we can expect miracles, and we will recognize His mighty hand in every situation.

*Meditate on the following:*

- *Saved by grace, what does that mean to me personally?*
- *Living in grace, how could I make that practical?*

*Journal your thoughts:*

# 12

*Growing in grace*

*Out of the fullness of his grace he has blessed us all,
giving us one blessing after another.*

**John 1:16**

We will recognize the mighty hand of God in every situation, like the apostle Paul did when he started off with telling the people in Corinth about the grace that God had given to the Macedonian churches (2 Corinthians 8).

It turned out they gave large gifts, much more than Paul expected, although they were poor. Paul recognizes the grace of God in this; the people could never have done that of their own accord. In verse 7 (NIV) he encourages the folks in Corinth to start living in that grace as well.

*But since you excel in everything—in faith, in speech, in knowledge, in complete earnestness and in the love we have kindled in you—see that you also excel in this grace of giving.*

Wow, they must have been a super church; somewhat like many churches around the world today, excelling in faith, speech, knowledge, earnestness, and love. Yet, they had been missing an important point: the grace of giving.

Paul urges them to use this gift from God. If we are serious in leaving the way of the thief behind and becoming true givers, we will need to use it just as much. Paul is gentle in his attitude towards the Corinthians; maybe he knew giving was a delicate subject. In 2 Corinthians 8:8 (NIV) he says,

*I am not commanding you, but I want to test the sincerity of your love by comparing it with the earnestness of others.*

Paul speaks the language of the Spirit, especially concerning God's law. He no longer barks God's commandments at his listeners: do this, don't do that, and shut up. No, he explains the new way of obeying God to them. It is no longer about obeying a set of rules; it is all about fulfilling them in a manner of love. Romans 7:6 sums up Paul's new way of looking at things,

*No longer do we serve in the old way of a written law, but in the new way of the Spirit.*

No longer is he trying to tell people what to do (remember that once he was a zealous Jew, a Pharisee, committed to the Law), no longer is he driven by the outward signs of religion. Instead of stuffing the Ten Commandments down people's throats, he urges people to change their minds, to obey God from the inside out, and to be sincere in their love for God and others. He measures the level of their giving with the sincerity of their love.

Paul experienced God's grace firsthand; he writes about it all the time. He saw God's grace in many aspects of life, not just in giving. Grace, God's free and unmerited favor, can be found throughout the history of mankind. The Bible talks about the spirit of grace, the message of grace, the grace of God, the throne of grace, and so on.

You may wonder how to actually live in that grace and how to benefit from it. How do you know if you have received God's grace? Listen,

*It is by God's grace that you have been saved.* (Ephesians 2:5)

God poured out his grace on mankind—on you and me. If it weren't for His grace, we wouldn't be here. God has showed us favor, even in times when we rebelled against Him, when we were still sinners. God poured out His grace on mankind when He gave up his Son as a sacrifice for our wrongdoing. Grace is invisible, yet it is evident in everything God has done for us. Second Timothy 2:1 tells us that grace is ours.

*As for you, my son, be strong through the grace that is ours in union with Christ Jesus.*

We can be strong in that grace which is ours in our union with Jesus. First of all, we have to be very serious in our relationship with Jesus. Just having Jesus as one of our acquaintances, along with many others, is not the unity the Bible speaks about. Unity involves a bond that cannot be broken, not even for a little while, for whatever excuse we have. Second of all, we have to exercise our walk in grace. Second Peter 3:18  says,

*Continue to grow in the grace and knowledge of our Lord and Savior Jesus Christ.*

We must continue to grow in the grace and knowledge of Him, just like Jesus and the early disciples did. It is not enough to accept God's gift of grace, say thank You, and store it with the rest of all our stuff. That would be the way of the thief. The Bible calls for a new lifestyle. We must turn away from our sinful lives and grow in grace. We have to grow in the grace by using it, giving it out, and, in doing so, multiplying it. Paul emphasized this in 2 Corinthians 6:1 (NIV):

*As God's co-workers we urge you not to receive God's grace in vain.*

We can tap into God's grace if we are sincere about becoming givers, the way Jesus had in mind when He spoke to the rich young guy. The man did not have the strength to do it; but then, he denied the invitation to become a disciple of Jesus. He was not in unity with Him; he wasn't willing to give it all. Is our attitude towards Jesus right? Is our commitment to live according to His teaching sincere? Jesus said in John 14:23,

*Whoever loves me will obey my teaching.*

We can become cheerful givers if we stop trying with our own strength. We have the example of Jesus, the help of the Holy Spirit, and the grace of God.

We can start off with self-disclosure. Check our attitude: see in what areas we are holding on to things. Evaluate our relationship with God. Is it a vibrant friendship, or are we bored with Him? Is honesty a basis in our relationship with Him? Reread the Scriptures that talk about giving and grace. Feed our spirit with Jesus's teaching by meditating on His words, by reading it aloud, and by talking things over with Him.

Last but not least, check our giving. Pray over our money, bless it, and give to God what belongs to Him. For starters, bring ten percent of our paycheck to the church or ministry that feeds us, our storehouse. We should do so before we spend it on anything else, and watch God at work. Be joyful in our giving, and we will notice we have entered that experience called grace.

So far, we have read how Jesus warns us in John 10:10 about the cunning ways of the thief. Furthermore, we read how He gave us everything we might possibly need so that we can have a life; the Bible calls it grace. It is by grace that we have received a new life (Romans 5:16-17).

Now it is time to take a closer look at the promise: a life in all its fullness.

**Meditate on the following:**

- *Am I growing in grace and knowledge of Jesus?*
- *How would I describe my new (Biblical) lifestyle?*

**Journal your thoughts:**

**Pray aloud:**

*Dear Father in heaven, thank you for giving up Your own Son so that I could have a life! Your grace is something I cannot grasp, but I want to walk in it and grow in it. I realize I am privileged to have Your power working in my life.*

*Holy Spirit, please guide me in the decisions I make every day. I have decided to become a true giver. What a wonderful example I have in Jesus, who came to give me life. I want to be in unity with Him.*

*In the name of Jesus, I ask this. Amen.*

# Part III

# The Promise

*...life in all its fullness!*

**John 10:10**

# 13

*Fullness of life*

*And you have been given full life in union with him.*

**Colossians 2:10**

In Part One of this book, we took a closer look at Jesus's warning against the ways of the thief. We learned that not stealing is merely obeying the Law. Fulfilling it in love is the next step. Jesus requires our action.

In Luke 6:38, He teaches us to become givers in order to receive the full measure back. His revolutionary teachings go against our human reasoning. In order to receive, we have to give first. In order to find, we have to lose. If we want to be first, we must become last. The way Jesus turns common sense upside down and inside out, sounds almost odd. It seems everything is always different from what we thought it to be in the first place. We have to keep adjusting our thinking.

In Part Two we saw how Jesus has set an example in giving. He gave His life for us so that we can have a life in all its fullness. He didn't say do this and that, and then I will give you a full life. We can never do anything to deserve that eternal life. It is grace that makes it accessible to us. Life in all its fullness is a gift from God to mankind. We also noticed that although this life is accessible for all God's children, we do not always experience it. We have to operate in that same grace in order to really experience what God has in mind for us.

Reading John 10:10 without reading the rest of Jesus's teachings would give the wrong picture. When Jesus promises us a life in all its fullness, we are not supposed to sit on the couch and wait for it to come. If that were true, we would have all experienced it a long time ago. Putting our faith in that promise means we need to activate our faith. Jesus spoke boldly about faith in John 14:12 (NIV) when he said,

*Very truly I tell you, whoever believes in me will do the works I have been doing, and they will do even greater things than these, because I am going to the Father.*

He didn't say, "Anyone who has faith in me needs to wait patiently for it to work." He clearly tells us to do what He has been doing. Within the context of our subject, that means give and it will be given to you, whether it is time, money, or love.

I want to emphasize the fact that we cannot do anything to deserve the promised life in all its fullness; it is by grace that we receive it. But in order to operate within that life and experience it to the full, we need to be in action. Let's say you have inherited a thousand acre property. It is yours; you have the ownership. In order to find out what kind of surprises that property has in store for you, you need to explore. Just staying at the entrance gate and telling everyone you own the place is not experiencing the full ownership; you merely acknowledge it.

You will have to explore the property to find out if there are forests, lakes, or mountains; if there is a place to develop; if there are trails to hike; if there is fruit to pick; etc. You have to start moving around the property. In the same way, we can only experience a life in all its fullness if we decide to start moving around. Just quoting that scripture will not bring us into the experience.

Now, Jesus did not require any special qualifications from us to enter that life, but we have seen in chapter three however that anyone who tries to enter the sheep pen in some other way than Jesus's way is a thief and a robber. We must leave the way of the thief behind and be willing to become givers, following in Jesus's footsteps.

That could have been the end of this book. I simply translated the letter of the Old Testament commandment into the new way of the Spirit. No longer does God command us; but the Spirit urges us from the inside out to fulfill the Law in love. We have been warned against the ways of the thief. We received His grace. Amen. End of story? No, Jesus adds the promise of a full life. What in the world does He mean when He talks about a life in all its fullness?

I would like to keep this as simple as possible. According to the Bible, a human life consists of three elements: spirit, soul, and body. We can find that in 1 Thessalonians 5:23,

*May the God who gives us peace make you holy in every way and keep your whole being—spirit, soul, and body—free from every fault at the coming of our Lord Jesus Christ.*

Our whole being is threefold. It is not surprising that we consist of three different elements, yet we are one person. God Himself is three—namely Father, Son, and Holy Spirit—and yet He is one. Genesis 1:27 tells us that, "God created human beings, making them to be like himself." Awesome! We will therefore look at fullness of our spirit, soul, and body. What does the Bible teach us about that?

First of all, the Bible makes it clear we have been given fullness in Christ (Colossians 2:10). Whatever worldly things we try to do to reach fullness will fail, because we can only get it through our relationship with Jesus. Fullness of life is a gift from God to mankind. We can never do anything to deserve it; it is grace. However, we must activate that promise in our lives.

Let us start with the fullness of our spirit. For most people, it is difficult to explain what our human spirit is. After all, a spirit is something supernatural, something invisible. Quite often, the human soul gets mixed up with the human spirit. The soul and the spirit must be close, maybe even tied together because the Bible says, "soul and spirit meet" (Hebrews 4:12). Now that is an interesting thought. Could it be that our soul interferes with our spirit? Could that be the reason we sometimes find it hard to tell if it is our soul or our spirit speaking in us? Is the so-called inner voice our soul or our spirit?

Many interesting books have been written about the soul and the spirit of man. I leave it up to you to further study the subject. I am not going to give Greek and Hebrew explanations either. In the next chapter, I simply want to explain what the Bible teaches us about the fullness of our spirit.

***Meditate on the following:***

- *What do I know about God?*

- *What does my spirit tell me about myself?*

***Journal your thoughts:***

# 14

## *Rebirth of the spirit*

*For you have been born again, not of perishable seed, but of imperishable, through the living and enduring word of God.*

**1 Peter 1:23 (NIV)**

Man was not a living being until the moment God gave him life by breathing on him. Genesis 2:7 (NIV) sounds somewhat poetic when it describes this creative miracle.

*Then the Lord God formed a man from the dust of the ground and breathed into his nostrils the breath of life, and the man became a living being.*

Man cannot live without the breath of life, which is spirit. Spirit equals breath. For more on this subject I would like to recommend my previous book, Breath of Life, which describes in detail how we become human beings. It is an artistic view of the melting together of spirit, soul, and body into one human being.

Man without breath is a mere body. Think about the end of Jesus's life on the cross. Luke 23:46 (NIV) says,

*Jesus called out with a loud voice, Father, into your hands I commit my spirit. When he had said this, he breathed his last.*

Matthew 27:50 says, "He gave up his spirit." In other words, the breath of life left him. Our spirit is the life we have in us. Without the spirit, without breath, we would be physically dead. Now, the spirit of man is more than just breath, it is also our wisdom and communication center. The Apostle Paul has a fine way of explaining a bit more about our human spirit, as he does in 1 Corinthians 2:11.

*It is only a person's own spirit within him that knows all about him; in the same way, only God's Spirit knows all about God.*

My spirit knows all about me, and God's spirit knows all about Him. That is wonderful, but how do we reach fullness of our spirit life? What does it mean that we can have fullness in union with Him? Is there more to our spirit than just breath, is there more to my spirit than just giving me life? The answer is yes!

The fullness of our spirit can be reached when we unite with God's Spirit. This is such an awesome miracle in God's creation; it blows me away every time I think about it. It is one thing to have my own spirit in me, who knows all about me; it is another thing to have God's

Spirit in me who knows all about God! The apostle Paul goes on to say in 1 Corinthians 2:12

*We have not received this world's spirit; instead, we have received the Spirit sent by God, so that we may know all that God has given us.*

'So that we may know all that God has given us.' We will know and understand through His Spirit; which is a learning process that might take a lifetime. I am sure, however, that having His Spirit will definitely bring us closer to knowing and understanding a life in all its fullness.

God gives us life by giving our bodies breath; let's call it the natural birth, our first birth. That way we can operate in the natural realm, we can communicate with other people. However, God desires to give us another life, which is called the second birth, by awakening our spirit and giving our spirit breath. That way, we can operate in the spiritual realm, we can communicate with God, who Himself is Spirit. Jesus explains this quite simply in John 3:6.

*A person is born physically of human parents, but he is born spiritually of the Spirit.*

He clearly speaks about two different kinds of birth: a physical birth and a spiritual birth. We need to experience both in order to receive fullness of life! No matter how good and wonderful our natural life is, it will never ever be complete until we become spiritually alive in Jesus Christ. I know this new birth, commonly referred to as being born again, is laughed at by many people who haven't experienced it.

It used to be complete hocus pocus to me until the day I surrendered; I gave my whole being over to God and I personally experienced the miracle of rebirth as explained in Romans 8:16,

*God's Spirit joins himself to our spirits to declare that we are God's children.*

Many seekers for spiritual enlightenment are, without realizing it, following the way of the thief. They think that by taking in education, meditation, and consultation, their spirits will develop. Although there is nothing wrong with educating and developing ourselves, something I would really encourage everyone to do, but by itself it means nothing. It should always be preceded by giving ourselves up to God.

We should not just take in; we must give out, or surrender, our spirit and ask God to unite with us. Jesus, for example, wanted to give the disciples the fullness of a spiritual life before He left the earth and He very clearly breathed the Holy Spirit on His disciples. John 20:22 says, "Then he breathed on them and said, 'Receive the

Holy Spirit'." Receiving God's Holy Spirit in us will make it possible to experience the fullness of life.

Fullness in spirit means we can learn as much as possible about God, we can communicate with Him, and we can hear His voice and learn His will for our lives. All too often, we feel the distance between God and man is awfully big. Could it be that we are trying to reach Him on our own accord, on our own conditions? Could it be that we never totally surrendered our spirit to His? Does the thief still rule over this part of your life? After all, it is possible to be a Christian and not have the Spirit of the living God in you.

In Ephesians 1:17, Paul prays for the believers and asks God to give them the Spirit. They had faith; they had love, but not the Spirit. Without the Holy Spirit, we are not complete. In the same way as the Church is not complete without acknowledging fullness of God in the Father, Son, and Spirit. It functions, but it does not experience fullness. Receiving God's Spirit in our lives is easy according to the Bible. In Luke 11:13 Jesus says,

*How much more, then, will the Father in heaven give the Holy Spirit to those who ask him!*

If you are not sure you have experienced spiritual rebirth, ask God the Father for it. It might help to read Paul's prayer as written down in Ephesians 1:15-17. He thanked God for the faith of the people in Ephesus, but wanted to make sure they all received the Spirit. He did not 'assume' they had received the Spirit just because they became believers, he asked for it!

*For this reason, ever since I heard of your faith in the Lord Jesus and your love for all of God's people, I have not stopped giving thanks to God for you. I remember you in my prayers and ask the God of our Lord Jesus Christ, the glorious Father, to give you the Spirit, who will make you wise and reveal God to you, so that you will know him.*

If you have decided to turn away from a sinful lifestyle and if you have faith in Jesus Christ it is no more than a logical step to ask Him for His Spirit to join yours. Believe me, spiritual rebirth is something you absolutely know for certain you have experienced, you just know that you know, that you know. Be honest in your prayer and receive in faith.

It is time to leave the ways of the thief behind, to give it all you've got. Jesus says, "Give and it will be given to you." We have to give our spirit to Him in order to be united with God's Spirit. The sixth and eighth chapter of the Book of Romans will explain this in more detail; giving up our spirit means dying to ourselves and dying to our old, sinful life only in order to receive a new and full life!

***Meditate on the following:***

- *Am I born again of the Spirit? Am I willing to testify in public?*

- *What has the Spirit done in my life?*

***Journal your thoughts:***

# 15



## *Emotional center*

*My soul is glad because of God my Savior*

**Luke 1:47**

As our spirit portrays the spiritual being we are and enables us to communicate with God, so our soul portrays the natural being we are, and enables us to communicate with other human beings. Our soul contains our emotions, intellect, mind, will, and imagination; we might call it our character.

I have based these words on what the Bible tells me about mankind, humanity, and the human soul. I must refer to the Bible to explain as simply as possible what our soul is and how we can obtain that fullness of life for our soul, since I have no scientific knowledge in this field. That doesn't bother me, because the Bible tells me in 1 Corinthians 1:20,

*So then, where does that leave the wise? or the scholars? or the skillful debaters of this world? God has shown that this world's wisdom is foolishness!*

I certainly do not want to criticize the world's wisdom, but this scripture encourages me to look for answers in the Bible, to not be afraid to study what God wants to teach me about the human soul, apart from all the books and studies that have been written in our world throughout history about this subject.

Reading through the Bible, we can find numerous scriptures about the soul. The soul is our emotional center. It is from deep down in our soul that happiness as well as bitterness, calmness, and anxiety come. Besides emotions, our soul realm holds strength, will-power, and knowledge too. Let's look at some scriptures.

- Our mind is indeed part of our soul; the Bible says our soul has knowledge. *Every one of you knows in his heart and soul that the Lord your God has given you all the good things that he promised* (Joshua 23:14).
- Our emotions are part of our soul. The condition of our soul impacts our behavior. *And she was in bitterness of soul, and prayed to the Lord and wept in anguish* (1 Samuel 1:10 NKJV).
- The condition of our soul changes. That is why it needs to be charged from time to time. Psalm 19:7 (NIV) says, *The law of the Lord is perfect, refreshing the soul.*

- Our ego is part of our soul. We can talk to our soul, Psalm 43:5 (NIV): *Why, my soul, are you downcast? Why so disturbed within me?*
- We can educate our soul, Proverbs 2:10 (NIV): *For wisdom will enter your heart, and knowledge will be pleasant to your soul.*
- We talk a lot about peace of mind, but let's not forget *rest for your souls*! As in Jeremiah 6:16 and Matthew 11:29 (NIV).

Our soul is a living part in us; it changes, it grows, and it can live or die. We are no robots; we have this emotional center that cannot be seen with the human eye. The soul symbolizes humanity, feelings, and emotions. Whether we cry, laugh, dance, or sing, it comes from within our soul. Somehow, our souls are not totally human business; God cares about our souls too. God himself has a soul, a character. God is one hundred percent divine, but He is not without emotions. Psalm 11:5 (NKJV) says,

*The Lord tests the righteous, but the wicked and the one who loves violence His soul hates*

God speaks similar words in Isaiah 1:14. Just look up the word soul in the concordance (that is a wordlist) of your Bible and you will find numerous interesting scriptures that will teach you more about our soul and God's soul.

Jesus, who came as God in human form, showed His emotions too. In Mark 14:34 (NIV) He cries out,

*My soul is overwhelmed with sorrow to the point of death.*

In Isaiah 53:11, we can find the prophecy about this suffering of Jesus's soul. God knows all about human souls. He made each human being with a unique character, and He wants to save that character together with our spirit. Yes, our souls can be saved; they don't have to go down the grave with our bodies. Jesus warns the people against losing their souls in Matthew 10:28 where He says,

*Do not be afraid of those who kill the body but cannot kill the soul; rather be afraid of God, who can destroy both body and soul in hell.*

God is in charge, but we choose. As I wrote in the previous chapters, the fullness of our spirit can be reached when we unite with God's Spirit. In other words, our spirit needs to be born again to reach that fullness. In the same way the fullness of our soul can be reached when it is saved (1 Peter 1:9) through our faith in Jesus and when we let Him be the overseer (1 Peter 2:25) of our soul.

Ever since I understood that the saving of my soul is not the same as the rebirth of my spirit, I stopped wondering how we would be able to recognize each other after we die, after we leave our earthly bodies behind. I know that many people who believe in eternal life are wondering how they will ever recognize loved ones outside this earthly realm. I studied that for the longest time and learned that as born again spirits we are all the same, namely as Jesus. 1 Corinthians 6:17 says,

*But he who joins himself to the Lord becomes spiritually one with him.*

As born again spirits we are all on the same level, since we are one with Him. I always thought that would be boring. Why would God make us all unique in the first place? Certainly not to scoop us all up in one big spiritual heap of robot Christians. He wants more than just born again spirits; He wants saved souls. I am slowly beginning to understand that I am a spirit being with a human soul, with certain characteristics. If my soul is saved, my emotions, my character, my uniqueness will be saved as well. So, I figure it is certainly possible to recognize our loved ones in heaven, we will know them by their character.

Our spiritual rebirth and the salvation of our soul are two different things that often happen at the same moment, but sometimes take place as separate events, as I will explain in the next chapter.

**Meditate on the following:**

- *How would I describe my soul?*

- *Can I say that my soul is saved? What does that mean to me?*

**Journal your thoughts:**

# 16

## *Salvation of the soul*

*You are receiving the salvation of your souls, which is the purpose of your faith in him.*

**1 Peter 1:9**

The salvation of our souls, our humanity, our character, is only possible through confession of faith in Jesus Christ. Don't ask me why that is the only way, it is how God has set it up, and because He is God, that settles it. John 3:16 is probably the most famous scripture about salvation,

*For God loved the world so much that he gave his only Son, so that everyone who believes in him may not die but have eternal life.*

It is no more complicated than that. We need to believe that in order to be saved. Remember again: do not try to climb in any other way, without showing yourself to the gatekeeper. It is absolutely essential to believe in the life, death, and resurrection of Jesus Christ. Paul had to explain the basics of salvation over and over during his ministry. In Romans 10:9-10 he says,

Actually, Paul clearly explains the difference between rebirth and salvation here. Being put right with God (by our faith), also called reconciliation, is our rebirth. Being saved (by our confession) is the salvation of our soul for eternity. Often, these two things do happen at the same time, but if we are not careful, it is easy to be mistaken about it. Think, for example, about the sinner on the cross next to Jesus. Because he called on the name of Jesus (confession), his soul was saved (Romans 10:13), but I don't think he ever truly experienced rebirth, simply because there was no time to live a redeemed life, lead by the Spirit of God.

Many people will say, "Well, Jesus saved my soul, I know that, but I am not experiencing fullness of soul. Often I am emotionally out of control; often I feel down or depressed." Now, this is where we sometimes have missed a point. Jesus is called the shepherd and overseer of our souls in 1 Peter 2:25. Just having our soul saved and continuing to live our way is not going to bring us fulfillment. Jesus wants to oversee our soul. He wants to keep an eye on us after we have been saved. He wants to shepherd us. Which basically means He wants to guide, correct, and take care of us. If we would let Him do that, we would find out that He is more than able to bring our soul to a fullness of life too.

Our soul needs to be shaped into fullness, because it has been poisoned by sin, pain, hurts, and corruption. Of course, it is wonderful to know that Jesus came to save our souls, but that is not all. He also wants to oversee, to shepherd our souls.  Let me explain the difference between spiritual rebirth and the salvation of our souls in another way. The moment we are born again, our spirit becomes one with the Lord and becomes new. Second Corinthians 5:17 explains this.

*When anyone is joined to Christ, he is a new being.*

Our soul, however, does not become new. On the contrary, it gets saved. We keep the same old soul with all its hurts, pains, and memories; that is why it needs shepherding, according to the Bible. Think again about John 10, the passage of scripture we used throughout this book, where Jesus explains His purpose on earth. He wants to be our good shepherd, not for one day, but forever. If we would let Him do that, we would start experiencing fullness of life for our soul. In John 10:17 Jesus takes His own life as an example for us when He says,

*The Father loves me because I am willing to give up my life, in order that I may receive it back again.*

God the Father loves us too. Are we willing to give up our life, our soul in order to receive it back again, this time in all its fullness? Just apply the main theme of this book here and ask yourself these questions: would I rather take than give? Do I keep my emotions to myself? Am I trying to preserve my ego? I am willing to give God my character, my humanity, for Him to oversee it? Do I mind being taken care of? Am I willing to accept guidance from God's Word, from Jesus's teachings? Can I take direction and correction?

The way of the thief simply means: not giving ourselves to God. It means keeping secrets and hanging on to hurts and habits. The enemy will use anything to keep us away from entering that fullness of life. Remember, he is a destroyer and a thief. God's will however, is life, life in all its fullness. The moment we decide to give Him all we've got—all of our emotions, all of our memories and all of our pain—He will bring balance, and we are on our way to enter that fullness of life Jesus talks about. Yes, when we are able to give our emotions to God, whether in praise or pain, in delight or despair, He will give us life.

Letting God oversee our soul seems a hard thing to do, we often struggle to let go of control. The eighth chapter of the Book of Romans teaches us however that we should be controlled by God's Spirit, and not by our human nature. In other words: the soul must be subject to the Spirit. Verse 9 says,

*But you do not live as your human nature tells you to; instead, you live as the Spirit tells you to—if, in fact, God's Spirit lives in you. Whoever does not have the Spirit of Christ does not belong to him.*

That is God's order for our life; spirit first, then soul, then body. Not the other way around. So, what can we do to surrender our soul to Him?

It means we have to be honest with Him and let go of shame. It means opening up our inner thoughts and feelings to Him, the way the psalmists did ever-so often. We can never ever do this without His Word. Often we seek the world's advice to soothe the pain in our soul. We try medication, counseling, indulging, shopping, over-eating, drugs and alcohol, self-pity, or whatever. Letting Jesus oversee our soul means we have to turn to the Bible for answers, for help. God gave us His Word for guidance.

Next time you feel distressed, anxious, or depressed, find words of encouragement and maybe even stories about similar situations to the one you are in. Learn from others and, best of all, read aloud God's promises. Talk to your soul, build it up, and let it be shaped by the Spirit through the living word. Next time you feel happy, relieved, or just excited; find words in the Bible you can use to express those feelings toward God. Find passages where people were filled with joy and danced and made music or gave offerings, learn from it, and give to God!

Apply the ancient words of the Bible and they will come alive; they will bring you life in all its fullness.

*Meditate on the following:*

- *Is everything well with my soul?*

- *How do I apply the Bible when dealing with my emotions?*

*Journal your thoughts:*

# 17



## *Feeding the flesh*

*Sin must no longer rule in your mortal bodies, so that you obey the desires of your natural self.*

**Romans 6:12**

When Jesus talks about a life in all its fullness, He doesn't just talk about our spiritual life. He talks about our physical, mental, emotional, relational, and financial life too. He talks about a full life in every area we can possibly think of.

Sometimes we have a tendency to over-spiritualize everything the Bible teaches and to forget that we have a natural life here on earth as well. Let's say you see someone in physical or material need and all you say is, "God bless you," and don't give him the necessities of life. What good is that faith? Faith without actions is dead (James 2:14-17). We can certainly apply this to the way we handle our own physical bodies.

When reading the biblical principles for a full life, we noticed that we can receive our true eternal life only through grace and faith in Jesus. In order to experience that life we have to activate our faith in it, not just sit and wait for it to come. The Bible tells us our spirits need to be born again and our souls need to be saved. What about our bodies? What part do our bodies have in the fullness of life?

Our bodies are temporary, the only thing about us that we will leave behind when we die. What can we do with our bodies to bring honor to God and to reach that fullness of life here on earth? Can our bodies add to the fullness of life? Are our bodies important to God, who is Spirit? The Bible says our bodies will turn to dust when we die (Genesis 3:19). Shouldn't we put all emphasis on the spirit and the soul? What did Jesus say about our bodies? Concerning the subject of this book: does the thief still rule or have access in our bodies? How can we give with our bodies?

Fullness of life means the rebirth of our spirit, the salvation of our soul and the sacrifice of our body.

Luke 22:19 contains an important statement of Jesus about the body, His body, when He eats the last meal together with His disciples. While breaking the bread He tells them,

*This is my body, which is given for you.*

In saying this Jesus again demonstrates His giving nature, which is in sharp contrast with the thief's way. Jesus gave His own body indeed to be tortured and abused so that we are able to go free. He gave up His body as a sacrifice for us and, in doing so, He has set the example for His followers. Not for us to die the same death, but to give up our bodies as a living sacrifice. Yes, the Bible calls for the sacrificing of our bodies. Romans 12:1 (NIV) puts it this way,

*Therefore, I urge you, brothers and sisters, in view of God's mercy, to offer your bodies as a living sacrifice, holy and pleasing to God—this is your true and proper worship.*

Note that Paul says living sacrifices. We are not asked to let ourselves be killed, although in many countries people are tortured and even murdered because of their faith in Jesus Christ. For most believers in the Western world this is not the case, and in general, we can say that God wants living sacrifices. Being a living sacrifice simply means giving up our body for the glory of God. Our bodies no longer belong to us; they belong to God, just as our spirits and souls belong to God. We purposely have to hand our whole beings over to Him, spirits, souls, and bodies, so He can begin and fulfill his work in us.

As Christians, we can experience healing, salvation, and deliverance in our whole being. Quite often our bodies get overlooked, because the term 'flesh' has a negative religious connotation. We don't want to put too much emphasis on our bodies, yet, we hardly ever find fullness in that area. We are either too thick, too thin, sick, weak, or undisciplined. Our bodies get poisoned with wrong foods, lack of exercise, (non) prescription drugs, pornography, etc. and we wonder why we do not experience fullness of life. Jesus offers us fullness of life; this certainly includes our physical being.

We have, however, on many occasions, been following the way of the thief, which is always more, more, more and me, me, me. Instead of taking good care of our bodies, which is after all the temple of the Holy Spirit; we have developed habits that are slowly destroying our earthly bodies. I think, to a certain extent, we are all guilty in some way of abusing our physical bodies. That can be changed, not through a diet or medication, but through the Word of God.

We are being asked to give our bodies up as an act of worship—an act of worship to God, not to the gods of fast food, alcohol, and drugs. This calls for surrender. In 1 Corinthians 6:19-20 the apostle Paul explains the biblical act of worship as follows:

*Don't you know that your body is the temple of the Holy Spirit, who lives in you and who was given to you by God? You do not belong to yourselves but to God; he bought you for a price. So use your bodies for God's glory.*

Paul clearly states that we need to be born again of the Spirit first, before being able to offer our bodies to God. He talks about people who have the Holy Spirit living in them. It is after that experience that we no longer belong to ourselves, but belong to God. Once the Spirit makes our body His home, we better do some serious cleaning so He can actually feel at home. Let me put it this way: if you are not happy living in your own body, why would the Spirit of the Living and Holy God feel welcome?

House cleaning is not such a bad task since the Spirit will help us; however, He is not going to do it all by Himself. It requires action from us. 1 Peter 1:14 says,

*Be obedient to God, and do not allow your lives to be shaped by those desires you had when you were still ignorant.*

See? It requires action. "Do not allow" means we have to take a stand. We need to change our attitude and our habits, and we need to get rid of sinful cravings in order to protect our bodies. It is so easy for sinful cravings to get out of control and become addictions, whether they are cravings for unhealthy food, alcohol, drugs, or sex. They will destroy us, given enough time, because they are the way of the thief and he has only one goal. So, what are we supposed to do?

I strongly believe that we no longer should go on thinking of ourselves as me, me, me, which basically means more, more, more as we have seen in this book. We have to learn to start thinking you, you, you Lord and no longer live to eat, drink, or indulge in order to satisfy our cravings. I fully understand that more, more, more and it's all about me are part of our modern-day culture, or should I say, that is our culture.

As believers, we might be living in that culture, but it is not ours. The apostle Paul writes in Romans 14:17,

*For God's Kingdom is not a matter of eating and drinking, but of the righteousness, peace, and joy which the Holy Spirit gives.*

We are part of a kingdom culture, which teaches us about giving as the Holy Spirit gives: to give cheerfully, to give abundantly, and to give it all.

It teaches us that if we hold on to things, we will eventually lose them. It teaches us that giving, not getting, is the way. Let us therefore make the decision to use our bodies for God's glory. We will start to reflect the full life He wants us to have. Yes, it is possible for all of us to reflect that fullness of life in our bodies as well, no matter what our physical appearance may be.

**Meditate on the following:**

- *Do I have bad habits, even addictions? Am I willing to take control with the help of the Holy Spirit?*

- *Do I feel at home in my body? Would the Holy Spirit feel welcome?*

**Journal your thoughts:**

# 18

## *Sacrifice of the body*

*This is why I tell you: do not be worried about the food and drink you need in order to stay alive, or about clothes for your body. After all, isn't life worth more than food? And isn't the body worth more than clothes?*

**Matthew 6:25**

Don't worry now; I am not going to say that everyone should go to the gym four times a week, hike the hills, run the beaches, and eat raw cabbage for dinner every night. I am not saying that we all have to fast every week or that we can never enjoy a rich meal anymore.

What I want to say is that we have to ask ourselves the following questions: would I rather take in or give out? Is my attitude towards my body still the way of the thief: always more, more, more? Do I want to be entertained, pampered, fed, and taken care of? Or am I willing to take care of my body in a way that makes me able to serve others? Jesus gave up his body for us; do we have anything to give to God or others?

Using our bodies for God's glory means that we have to keep them clean and strong in every possible way. Each person is different, so there is no standard way to do this. It is between us and God. The Bible calls for holy and clean living. I realize I am treading on dangerous ground when writing about the maintenance of our bodies, yet the Bible speaks about it quite frankly. In Proverbs 23:20-21 for example, we are told to stay away from drunkenness and gluttony!

I have seen that obesity is a huge problem in the USA, bigger than in any other country in the world that I've visited. At the same time, I noticed it is a very delicate subject, even within Christian circles. Most people do not like to talk about it in a serious way and I even noticed that overeating is subject to many jokes and countless giggles. Does God love you when you are overweight or undisciplined or have an addiction? Yes, of course, He does, but He urges us to stop giving in to our own desires all the time.

I personally believe we have to be as serious about our addictions and bad habits as God is. As long as we treat obesity, for example, as something that will go away if we regulate it by means of a diet, we are wrong. It would be like telling an alcoholic to drink only a small amount of alcohol each day and only splurge on weekends or birthday parties. It would be like telling a heroin addict to take smaller portions and to count the grams of intake.

Let's stop fooling ourselves and start building clean, strong, and beautiful temples for the Holy Spirit to live in. Let's no longer treat our disorders as funny but let us surrender our bodies to Christ. 2 Peter 2:19 says,

*For we are slaves of anything that has conquered us.*

Admitting our weaknesses opens the door to recovery. We can make the decision that sin will no longer rule in our bodies, whatever sin that may be. God will take over with his Holy Spirit who produces self-control in us, as mentioned in Galatians 5:23. What a comfort. Even in conquering our habits and hang-ups the Holy Spirit is there to help. We are never alone. When we make the decision to offer ourselves up for Him, and truly mean it, everything will change. We will leave behind the way of the thief. Offering our bodies as a living sacrifice means that we are available to God; available for Him to use us. I believe that as long as we have to fight battles in our bodies, it will be hard to help others. For starters, we are not being good examples to nonbelievers or new Christians.

It is easy to see how we have become unbalanced in obtaining fullness of life. Some people are mainly emotional beings, always going by feelings, always driven by emotions (I feel like, I wish, I could, I should). Some people are mainly spiritual beings. All they ever talk about is God and the Bible. They soak in His word and devour His teachings; but they never give out, they never help others, they never try to understand the person on another level. Some people indulge in the body or flesh. All they ever talk and think about is cravings; they are always either shopping or eating, or drinking or vacationing. They indulge, they take in, and they stuff themselves (literally) to numb the soul and quiet the spirit. Are you in any of these groups? Do not hesitate to seek help and encouragement from someone who seems to have conquered the same area you struggle with.

In regards to our bodies, we must learn to become givers too. For example, when we fast, we humble ourselves; we give ourselves to God. When we exercise, we take care of what He has entrusted us with, we give Him our thanks in a practical way. When we get rid of sin, we give our weaknesses to Him. When we conquer a habit, we give Him the glory. I realize every single person on earth is different and we all have different shapes and sizes; that is the uniqueness of God's creation. We are not supposed to try to look like someone else. We are asked to take care of our own bodies.

God will help us, but we have to be willing to make a start. Let's leave the way of the thief behind, which is always calling for more, more, and more. His way will lead to destruction, but Jesus's way will lead to life, a balanced life, a life in all its fullness.

Being a believer equals fullness of life. If that is not true, then John 10:10 is not true. I believe we can all experience whole-life abundance as mentioned and promised in John 10:10. We need to activate our faith in that promise and come into action. We have to become givers, following in Jesus's footsteps. He has set the stage by giving the ultimate gift: His very own life! He did this in order that we might have life in all its fullness. Romans 6:12-14 is a wonderful Scripture that sums up everything we talked about in this book; it talks about the surrender of our whole being to God. It is so encouraging.

*Sin must no longer rule in your mortal bodies, so that you obey the desires of your natural self. Nor must you surrender any part of yourselves to sin to be used for wicked purposes. Instead, give yourselves to God, as those who have been brought from death to life, and surrender your whole being to him to be used for righteous purposes. Sin must not be your master; for you do not live under law but under God's grace.*

Wow, what a Scripture; it talks about Part One, Two, and Three of this book: getting rid of sin (stop following the ways of the thief), the grace of God (He will always help us, He gave it all) and complete surrender of our whole being (promise of a life in all its fullness). Let's check every area of our being and ask ourselves if we have truly given it up for Him. The Bible urges us to:

- *Give up our spirit to become one with God's spirit.*
- *Give up our soul to be saved and shepherded by Jesus.*
- *Give up our body as a living sacrifice for God's glory.*

We are indeed talking about a complete surrender here—a surrender with all of our spirit, all of our soul, and all of our body. If we sincerely decide to live life Jesus's way, the biblical way, instead of finding all kinds of excuses to do it our way, we will experience that fullness of life.

The thief will no longer be able to steal from us what the Lord has promised!

*__Meditate on the following:__*

- *Am I willing to surrender my whole being to God?*

- *How can I use my body for God's glory?*

*__Journal your thoughts:__*

**Pray aloud:**

*Dear Father in heaven, thank You for giving me a body to live in. Thank You for making me in Your image, for Your willingness to share Your Holy Spirit with me. Thank You Jesus for giving up Your body as a sacrifice for me, I can be free. Thank You for being the shepherd of my soul.*

*Holy Spirit, please help me to control my cravings and habits. Show me where I need guidance and help. I want to be able to glorify Jesus with my whole being; I want to walk, sing, dance, and run for Him.*

*From now on, I am no longer a slave; I am free! I thank You for the promise of a life in all its fullness. I can enjoy it now! Thank You.*

*In Jesus's name, I pray this. Amen.*

# Conclusion

*No one takes my life away from me. I give it up of my own free will.*

**John 10:18**

Well, I did write a book about three words. Do not steal; that is where we started, and that is where we will end. God has a life in all its fullness in store for you, don't let anyone steal that from you and don't steal from God.

Every so often, we turn out to be the thieves of our own happiness by not giving it all up for God. The more we want to keep for ourselves, the unhappier we will be; that is the way of the thief. The way of the Master however is excellent and true,

*Give to others, and God will give to you. Indeed, you will receive a full measure, a generous helping, poured into your hands—all that you can hold. The measure you use for others is the one that God will use for you* (Luke 6:38) .

It all starts with giving; and in order to use the right measure we should start with giving ourselves to God. When we surrender all of our being to God, we will soon find out that it becomes easier and easier to be a giver in all areas of life, whether it is about money, time, talents, love, or practical help.

There is no seven-steps plan to become a cheerful giver; it requires a change from the inside out, a change in our whole being. The Bible calls for 'cheerful giving,' which is certainly possible, whether we are rich or poor. It has nothing to do with your bank accounts, but it has everything to do with the condition of our heart.

It is one thing to say we are not a thief; it is another thing to become a giver. That is a whole new level!

# Bibliography

Also available in English:

**True Worshipers**, *Answering the Father's call for a lifestyle of pure devotion* (2020)

We never thought it could happen in just a few weeks, certainly not on a worldwide scale. But it did. Our churches had to close their doors, although temporarily, due to government regulations in response to a virus epidemic.

That brings us to a realistic and probing question. What would be left of our modern-day Christianity when all is taken away: the buildings, the meetings, the money, the power, the titles, the theology, the music, and the concerts? What would be left? We might find ourselves on our knees again, without anything. No effects, no band, no structure, no liturgy to follow. Just us, on the floor… waiting for God to speak, waiting for Him to come. After more than two thousand years of Christianity we might find ourselves bowing down again, empty-handed, with nothing but our time and lives to give Him.

Jesus prophesied that the time was coming when by the power of God's Spirit people would worship the Father as He really is, offering Him the true worship He so desires. Have you ever wondered what true worship would be like? It begins where idolatry ends. Yes, it will take a powerful move of the Holy Spirit to have our institutionalized Christianity make the transition into relational Christianity. And yes, this process starts in the heart of every believer. Will you answer the Father's call for a lifestyle of pure devotion?

**In My Name**, *Inviting God's holy presence in daily situations* (2018)

It is one thing to claim we don't use the Lord's name in vain, but what do we do? Are we bringing honor to His name? Do we have a genuine love for His name? And most of all, is everything we do and say then, done in His name? The letter of the Old Testament law says 'do not use the Lord's name in vain', Jesus however urges every believer to 'honor His holy name'. We will find out how such a commandment can become practical and applicable for believers today, not by focusing on what we cannot and should not do, but by focusing on what the Holy Spirit wants to do in us and through us. May we use God's name with power, purpose and reverence in effective ministry all over the world and in doing so be a generation that fulfills the ancient scriptures right here and now in the 21st century.

**Spirit of Truth,** *Finding certainty and standing firm in a troubled world* (2016)

One of the most famous questions ever asked in the history of mankind, was the one Pilate desperately confronted Jesus with: 'and what is truth?' In Spirit of Truth the reader is being challenged to answer Pilate's question and to go on a quest for that one certainty that would settle all dispute, all error, all doubt: Truth, with a capital T. Find out the importance of living and speaking truthfully and discover how to stand up for biblical values and principles in a troubled world that seems to have taken a free fall into lawlessness.

**My Neighbor's House,** *Digging Deeper to Find the Treasure That will Satisfy the Longing of Your Heart* (2013)

What do we do with the old pages of Exodus 20 in this current age and time? How do we apply them in our daily life? It is one thing to say, "Oh, I don't envy my neighbor, his house, car, or wife. I don't desire what someone else has." But come to think of it, what do you desire? What are the desires of your heart? Are you passionate for the right things? In this fifth book in the Ten Commandments series, you'll learn how to desire meaningful things and apply God's word to everyday life.

## **Grace of Giving**, *Turning the Key to Enter & Experience Fullness of Life* (2011)

**2011 Reader's Favorite Gold Medal Award Winner**
**'Best Christian Non-Fiction'**

It is one thing to claim we do not steal, but the logical next question would be, "What do we do? How do we go from merely obeying such a command to fulfilling it in our daily lives? Is it truly possible to become a cheerful giver?" In her award-winning book Grace of Giving, the fourth one in this series, Marja answers these questions by taking an in-depth look at the commandment "do not steal." The author offers a liberating and fresh insight on the eighth commandment as she shares how we can leave behind the way of the thief, which always cries for more, more, more. In her known step-by-step method, she slowly reveals the way of the Master, which is cheerful, abundant, and costly giving that will lead us into a life in all its fullness!

## **Breath of Life**, *A Journey into Origin and Purpose of Spirit, Soul, and Body* (2008)

As human beings, we are made in the image and likeness of God. We are uniquely designed triune beings: spirit, soul, and body, yet one. The author takes the reader on a journey to our earthly beginnings and beyond. Based on biblical concepts and a surprising array of scriptures, she has painted an artistic picture of a colorful and loving God who is the source of all life. Breath of life is based on the commandment not to commit murder and it deals with the very core of our existence: life before and after conception.

## **Respectfully Yours**, *Revealing God's Truth about Well-being and a Long Life* (2007)

Respectfully Yours is the second book in a series about the Ten Commandments in the twenty-first century. Based on the commandment to honor our parents, it deals with a much broader aspect of family life—the mutual respect between God, parents, and children. The letter of the Old Testament bursts into life as author Marja explains the new way of the Spirit. This book is not just a short and easy-to-understand study; it is a thought-provoking page turner that will transform your view of the parent-child relationship!

## **Sacred Sabbath**, *God's Way to Multiply Our Time and Restore Our Joy* (2006)

Sacred Sabbath is the first book in a series about the Ten Commandments in the twenty-first century. It is a short and easy to understand study that doles out profound nuggets of wisdom to anyone who wants to live the life God had in mind when He created mankind. It explains how we can fulfill The Law in a spirit of love just as

Jesus did. Sacred Sabbath will lead the reader into an inward change rather than toward an outward experience.

**End notes**

The Penguin English Dictionary, second edition, © the Estate of G.N. Garmonsway, 1965, 1969, made and printed n great breitain by hazell Watson & Viney Ltd, Aylesbury, Bucks.


Visit the author at www.marjameijers.com